THE GREAT
SANDWICH BOOK

Other books by Anita Borghese

The Down to Earth Cookbook
The Complete Book of Indonesian Cooking (co-author)
The International Cookie Jar Cookbook
Foods from Harvest Festivals and Folk Fairs
Just Desserts

THE GREAT SANDWICH BOOK

**The Relaxed Way to Entertain
for Brunch, Lunch, Picnics,
Cookouts, Snacks, Teatime,
Cocktails, and More**

ANITA BORGHESE

Rawson Associates Publishers, Inc., New York

The quotation from "Yes, But Can the Steam Engine Do This?", from GETTING EVEN, by Woody Allen, © copyright 1966, 1967, 1968, 1969, 1970, and 1971 by Woody Allen, is reprinted by permission of Random House, Inc.

Library of Congress Cataloging in Publication Data

Borghese, Anita
The great sandwich book.

Includes index.
1. Sandwiches. I. Title.
TX818.B67   641.8'4   77–15807
ISBN 0–89256–049–5
ISBN 0–89256–060–6 pbk.

Designed by Joyce Weston
First edition

TO JOHN
For all the best reasons

ACKNOWLEDGMENTS

For their kind sharing of recipes, theories, or techniques my sincere thanks to: Josette Passarelli, Carmen and Marifé Garcia, Frances Klein Schoen, Robert Pinart, Margaret Perkins of Moreton-on-Marsh, England, Dorothy Bagg, Margaret Eddy, Bennetta Fajardo, Maria Castro, Florinda and Valerie Marona, Hazel B. Daigle, George H. Gartner of *New Orleans Magazine*, and John Perrone of Progress Grocery Co., New Orleans, La.

—ANITA BORGHESE
Pleasantville, New York
November 1977

CONTENTS

THE GREAT
SANDWICH BOOK

1. THE SANDWICH YESTERDAY AND TODAY

He freed mankind from the hot lunch. We owe him so much.
—WOODY ALLEN, Getting Even. *"Yes, But Can the Steam Engine Do This?"*

What makes the sandwich so popular today is its amazing versatility. The sandwich family includes members of all shapes and sizes, from the great-grand-daddy-size Reuben that fills an entire plate to tiny cock-tail or tea sandwiches an inch in diameter that make up in tang and flavor what they lack in size. A good sandwich is a thing of beauty and a delicious yet honest and straightforward food, since its base, bread, is the staff of life.

The intent of this book is to explore with you the remarkable world of the sandwich today, a food to serve you around the clock in all seasons of the year.

Where Did the Sandwich Come From?

No one really knows for sure who invented the sandwich, but the theories about its beginnings are fascinating to ponder.

History credits Hillel, a famous and learned rabbi who lived at the time of Herod, with having started the Passover custom of sandwiching a mixture of chopped nuts, apples, spices, and wine between two matzohs to eat with bitter herbs as a reminder of the suffering of the Jews before their deliverance from Egypt. The filling between the matzohs represented the mortar used by the Jews in their forced labor of constructing Egyptian buildings and similar works. While this symbolic food cannot be thought of as everyday fare, it is probably the world's first recorded sandwich, and one that is eaten at Passover time to this day.

Some thousands of years later, in the Middle Ages, came what we might think of as the first open-faced sandwich. Eaters of those days, when plates were expensive commodities, substituted thick blocks of bread called trenchers, piling meat and other foods on top. At the end of the meal, one either ate the trencher or, if hunger had been assuaged, tossed the gravy-soaked slab to another less fortunate, human or canine. Though trenchers are a thing of the past, the word "trencherman"—someone with a hearty appetite—reminds us today of this early version of the modern open-faced sandwich.

And long before England's fourth Earl of Sandwich hit upon the idea of using two slices of bread to hold meat slices and thus keep his hands grease- and fork-free during his card-playing binges, the Arab world had been savoring envelopelike sandwiches of pita bread stuffed with succulent bits of barbecued meat. While his lordship was thus immortalized in lending his name to the sandwich, we should remember that the pita-stuffers were the first to come up with the idea of a practical, pleasing, and nearly leak-proof sandwich.

It seems likely too that in various parts of the Western world many centuries ago, peasants working in the field halted their labors at high noon to consume lunches of bread and cheese eaten in sandwich fashion, and it is pleasant to think of their simple midday repasts as the first picnic sandwiches.

We know for certain that across the Atlantic, even before the time of the Aztecs, peoples in ancient Mexico made corn tortillas, stuffed them with various kinds of vegetable, meat, and fruit fillings, and rolled them up to form crêpelike sandwiches.

No matter where or when the first sandwich may have been made, it is, happily for us, here to stay. Today we can choose the best sandwiches from cuisines all over the world, and a wide array of foods with which to make them. The diversity of the sandwich in America makes it not only an appropriate but an outstanding type of food for every meal, for any occasion, for any time of day or night. What else serves so well as the mainstay of almost any meal?

Sandwiches through the Day—And into the Night

Starting with the first meal of the day, the sandwich is just as much at home at the brunch or breakfast table as ham and eggs or a bowl of cereal—but so much more inspired. The sandwich rules supreme at lunch time in homes, offices, restaurants, schools, and just about everywhere else. Whether you're a construction worker eating your lunch on a steel girder a thousand feet up in the sky or a business executive munching at ground level, what you want is a sandwich when the twelve-o'clock whistle blows.

Sandwiches are great snacks and perfect between-meal treats. At midnight, when everyone else is sleeping, it's such a delight to tiptoe to the refrigerator and put together a tantalizing sandwich.

Sandwiches are nice at supper time, too, when a heavy meal is out of place—especially on a Sunday when everyone has had an ample midday dinner and wants something light for the day's last meal. And the cocktail hour, one of the day's most pleasant times, is when tempting little bite-size sandwiches make taste buds tingle.

And then there's teatime. Whether it's tea for two or for twenty, sandwiches are called for as surely as bread calls for butter. Tea and sandwiches, born companions, were the first types of sandwiches to evolve from the Earl of Sandwich's first crude prototype for what was to become a lifestyle in eating.

There are all sorts of surprisingly good brunch sandwiches in Chapter 5 that are guaranteed to wake up morning appetites. Have Mexican-inspired Huevos Rancheros on Tortillas or English-inspired Crabs on Crumpets, only two of the many good ways to begin the day with a sandwich.

Lunch-time sandwiches, in Chapter 4, offer a variety you may never have considered, and the menu suggestions at the end of most recipes will help make your lunch nutritionally balanced and attractive. For example, the Syrian Special is pita bread filled with a tempting hot mélange of ground lamb and tomatoes perfumed with parsley, lemon, allspice, and other seasonings. Or you may prefer an open-faced lip-smacker like German Liverwurst Caprice, which combines pumpernickel and crispbread in the same sandwich. The ideas are many, the preparation not difficult, and all will give new life to lunch time.

If your lunch time turns into picnic time, turn to Chapter 6 and see how much fun a picnic can be with an Endless Hero (any number can eat), a basket of earthy European Workmen's Sandwiches and a jug of red wine, or a truly showoff Picnic Sandwich à la Russe. While you're thinking of the outdoors, look over the recipes in Chapter 7 for your next cookout. If you're bored with burgers and fed up with franks, then throw another log on the fire and start to make some Curried Shrimp in Crisp Coconut Rolls. On the other hand, if you wish there was a really *different* hot dog or hamburger, then Chorizo Dogs and Sesame Vealburgers are the answer.

Before consigning your waffle iron to the next tag sale in your neighborhood, wait until you've tried a Waffled Soho Sandwich, among the many goodies in store for you in Chapter 8. In addition, you'll find gorgeous Danish Open-faced Sandwiches you'll be proud to serve to late-evening guests, a Lashing Tongue Sandwich to keep everyone else quiet while you get a chance to do some talking, and a Nutted Tuna and Spinach Sandwich perfect for a Sunday-night supper.

Small appetizing sandwiches in Chapter 9 will give new flair to your sandwich tray at cocktail time. Grilled

Chutney Cheese Sandwiches are good hot, nippy treats, and Boursin Omelet Bites are bound to bring compliments. If you want to do most of your preparation ahead and serve cold cocktail sandwiches, then think about Sweet Red Italian Onion Sandwiches, which are easy on the budget even as the sandwiches disappear by the dozens.

Some Practical and Nutritious Things About Sandwiches

Sandwiches are right for every occasion and time, but there are lots of other reasons why they've become a "must" food across the nation. One of the best is the truly dazzling variety of breads available: lusty loaves of whole-grain breads, crusty rolls and long loaves, pita breads with their built-in pockets for stuffing, and scores of ethnic breads. Chapter 3 gives recipes for many of these wonderful breads for those who want to bake their own, either for the sheer joy of baking or because certain breads are not available in their area. There are recipes for unusual breads that make novel and delicious sandwiches. Chappati is one such bread, speedy to make and not sold in stores.

You'll find most of the sandwich recipes here easy to do and many are very quick, although a few will keep you happily cooking for a longer time when leisurely cooking is your aim. Whether simple or elegant, all have superb flavor, with recipes geared to suit all budgets (and a general aim at keeping ingredients reasonably priced). Much of the work can be done ahead of time, for assembling or cooking at the last minute. Many sandwiches, such as those in the picnic chapter, can be completely made ahead. These recipes let you budget your time, so you can be with your guests instead of in the kitchen while everyone else is having a good time.

The many people who today are interested in cutting down their meat intake, for reasons of health or ecology, will be delighted by recipes for sandwiches that use eggs, fish, cheese, and combinations of vegetables for the filling. The Pisto de Aragón Sandwich, for example, is a hot, fragrant combination of vegetables lightly bound together with egg and spooned into hollowed-out hard rolls. (For your convenience, all such sandwiches are listed in the Index under "Meatless Sandwiches.")

Be sure not to overlook the final chapter in this book, which tells all about garnishes and pickles, including recipes for many exotic pickles and chutneys that you probably can't find in stores. Garnishes make sandwich plates and platters extra pleasing to look at.

Take time to read Chapter 2 before you start, and have a wonderful time traveling through the world of sandwiches. I did!

2. BEFORE YOU BEGIN: A Word about the Recipes

Good beginnings make good endings.
—*French proverb*

ABOUT THE SANDWICH RECIPES

Proportions: Where set proportions of sandwich ingredients are desirable, exact quantities are stated in the recipes and should be adhered to. For example, for the Souffléed Cheddar Sandwich the amount of the ingredients should not be altered if the sandwich is to puff properly.

However, where quantity of filling is obviously a matter of personal preference, you need not be bound by suggested amounts. For instance, there are no set proportions for how many slices of salami or provolone make a perfect hero sandwich, but the Hero recipe here suggests a quantity for the average taste. **Yield:** The number of sandwiches that a recipe yields is stated at the end of the recipe. If you wish to make twice as many sandwiches, simply double all ingredients.

Special ingredients: Most all of the ingredients in the recipes are easily obtainable at supermarkets, grocery stores, and bakeries. A few special ingredients can be found in more specialized food stores; in such cases, suggested sources are given with the individual recipe. Several recipes call for tahini (ground sesame seed) and the optional ingredients tamari soy sauce and miso (soy-bean paste). These three items can be bought in health-food stores and in some supermarkets and specialty food stores.

Toasting one side of bread slices: When a recipe calls for toasting bread on one side only, arrange the bread slices on a baking sheet and put it under the broiler until the bread is toasted. Remove from the oven and proceed with the recipe.

Menu Suggestions: After most of the sandwich recipes you will find suggestions for foods that go nicely to round out a menu. Recipes for some of the suggested accompaniments and salads can be found by consulting the Index.

ABOUT THE BREAD RECIPES

Baking powder: In a recipe calling for baking powder you may use any type of baking powder you like unless it specifically calls for double-acting baking powder.

Yeast: All recipes using yeast call for packaged active dry yeast. If using loose active dry yeast, substitute 1 level tablespoon active dry yeast for 1 package active dry yeast.

Flour: All recipes that call for whole wheat flour are best made with stone-ground whole wheat flour. If this is not available, use ordinary whole wheat flour. In the same vein, the preferred white flour is unbleached, simply to do away with unnecessary consumption of chemicals, but if you wish you can use ordinary white flour.

Warm water: When recipes call for "warm water, about 115°," you can judge the temperature without a thermometer by dropping the water on the inside of your wrist. It should be comfortably warm but not hot enough to hurt—somewhat like the temperature of milk heated for a baby's bottle.

ABOUT ALL THE RECIPES

Butter: Any recipe that calls for butter can be made with margarine unless the recipe specifically states that substitutes are not acceptable.

Eggs: All eggs used in these recipes are medium-size.

Grated orange or grated lemon peel: Grate only the outer orange or yellow part of the fruit peel or rind (the zest). Be certain not to include any of the white part of the peel, which has a bitter taste.

Cucumbers: Peel cucumbers if they have been waxed. Otherwise do not peel cucumbers unless the recipe specifically calls for them to be peeled.

Mushrooms: All mushrooms used in these recipes are fresh mushrooms.

Washing vegetables and fruits: All vegetables and fruits should be washed, dried, and, where necessary, trimmed before their use in any recipe.

Temperatures: All cooking and baking temperatures are in Fahrenheit. To convert to Centigrade (Celsius) subtract 32 from the Fahrenheit temperature and divide the result by 1.8.

3. GREAT BEGINNINGS:
Breads, Butters, and Mustards

"A loaf of bread," the Walrus said,
"Is what we chiefly need."
—LEWIS CARROLL, *Through the Looking-Glass.*

Start off with a worthwhile bread and your sandwiches are bound to be good. There are so many kinds of alluring, mouth-watering breads available nowadays that there's no reason to settle for less than a super sandwich. What was once unusual or exotic has now become commonplace. Pita bread (sometimes called Middle Eastern bread or sandwich pockets), for example, was virtually unknown a few years ago. Now it's on the bread shelf in supermarkets nearly everywhere.

Whole-grain breads are found in increasing and seemingly infinite variety in every food store. Bakery shops and delicatessens dispense tempting rolls, buns, and breads of all kinds. Department stores with bakery counters display an ever-increasing selection of loaves of many ethnic origins, ranging from braided challah to Lithuanian pumpernickel.

Unusual packaged breads are sold through supermarkets and chain stores with, for example, New York's Munzenmaier Baking Co. supplying a great number of pumpernickels and dark breads and Chicago's Rubschlager Baking Corp. turning out Swedish lympa and French sourdough bread along with many pumpernickels and ryes. There are also a good many whole-grain breads carefully wrapped in airtight heavy foil and imported from Scandinavia and Germany. Many of these are available in both regular-size loaves and in rounds or squares just right for cocktail sandwiches. San Francisco is famous for its tangy, crusty sourdough bread, now shipped all over the country. Italian bakeries sell not only white but whole wheat loaves in all sizes and shapes, with and without sprinklings of sesame seeds.

Chances are you won't be able to get all of these breads in every area of the United States, but you will be able to get many of them, and a careful look at what's at hand in local bake shops and supermarkets will probably surprise you—there's bread all around you.

But even if you can buy a particular bread, you will enjoy making your own for a change. What sandwich could be better than one made with your own freshly baked bread, and what aroma is more heavenly than that of bread baking in the oven?

The following are recipes not only for individual

breads, such as pita, chappati (a flat bread which originated in India, makes a sturdy sandwich base, and is easily made on a griddle on top of the stove), and whole wheat hamburger rolls (a nice change from the usual white variety), but loaves of pumpernickel, rye, Swedish lympa, challah, and many others with flavorings of cheese, dill, or tomato to enhance any sandwich that might come to mind. There are also several recipes for fruit breads that make nice tea sandwiches and out-of-the-ordinary picnic sandwiches.

At the end of each bread recipe you will find a list of sandwich recipes in which the particular bread is utilized, but feel free to use any of the breads in any sandwich that pleases you. You can't do anything but have a great sandwich adventure.

After the bread recipes in this chapter you'll find recipes for sandwich butters and clarified butter, as well as a discussion of all the delicious mustards to use in your sandwiches.

PITA BREAD

This method, discovered after much trial and error, turns out puffy pita every time. Just follow the directions exactly and nothing will go wrong. The secret for success is in rolling the dough to the proper thickness, allowing it to rise to the proper thickness, and baking it in the center of a very hot oven on a heated greased baking sheet.

1 package active dry yeast
1¼–1½ cups warm water, about 115°
⅛ teaspoon sugar
4 cups white flour
½ teaspoon salt
2 teaspoons vegetable oil

Sprinkle yeast over ¼ cup of the warm water and stir until yeast is dissolved. Add sugar and set in a warm place until mixture begins to become foamy, about 5 minutes. Meanwhile, sift flour and salt together into a bowl. Make a well in the center and add yeast mixture. Mix well, adding enough of the warm water to make a slightly firm but not stiff dough. Turn out on floured board and knead about 15 minutes, working in the oil a teaspoon at a time, until smooth and elastic. Place in oiled bowl; turn dough over to make sure it is oiled all over. Cover bowl with plastic wrap and set in a warm place to rise until double in bulk, about 2 hours.

Punch down dough and knead again on floured board a few minutes. Divide dough into 6 or 8 equal parts. Flatten and shape each with the hands into patty shape. Dust each with flour and roll out on floured board with floured rolling pin to exactly ¼ inch thickness. Measure with a ruler. This is an important step and not as easy to judge as it may seem. Place a clean dish towel on a tray or board and sprinkle with flour. Lay rolled-out pitas on towel, leaving spaces in between. You will need 2 or 3 trays for this operation. Cover pitas with another clean towel sprinkled with flour, the flour rubbed in. Allow to rise in a warm place until exactly ½ inch high, again measuring with a ruler. This rising will take 30–45 minutes.

Meanwhile, place oven rack in center of oven. You will be baking only one pan at a time unless you have a huge oven. Preheat oven at 500°. A minute or two before ready to bake, place a greased baking sheet in the oven. When it is very hot, but not smoking, remove it and place 2 or 3 pitas on it. Bake about 6 minutes. Watch carefully so that they do not scorch. Remove from baking sheet and cool on wire rack. With a brush (not a nylon brush, which will melt) regrease the baking sheet and continue baking the pitas. If not using the pitas immediately, or on the day of baking, wrap in plastic wrap before completely cooled and refrigerate or freeze. Unwrap and heat in oven until just heated through. It will only take a few minutes.

Makes 6–8.

WHOLE WHEAT PITA BREAD

Prepare as for Pita Bread, above, with the following exceptions:

Substitute 3 cups whole wheat flour and 1 cup white flour for the 4 cups white flour.

Decrease the amount of vegetable oil to 1½ teaspoons.

The first rising will take less time than the white-flour pita; it can take as little as 1 hour and 15 minutes.

Reduce the baking time by about 1 minute.

SANDWICH SUGGESTIONS: Big Raw Vegetable Pillows, Piperade Pita, Syrian Special, Tofu-Shrimp Stuffed Pita, Turkish Shish Kebob in Pita Bread

CRUSTY WHOLE WHEAT HAMBURGER ROLLS

1 package active dry yeast
1 cup warm water, about 115°
1 tablespoon sugar
2 tablespoons melted butter or margarine,
    cooled
2 tablespoons instant nonfat dry milk
    powder
1 teaspoon salt
1 cup white flour
2 cups whole wheat flour
1 egg, beaten

Sprinkle yeast over ¼ cup of the warm water in a large bowl and stir until yeast is dissolved. Add ½ teaspoon of the sugar and stir again. Set in warm place until mixture begins to become foamy, about 5 minutes. Add balance of sugar and water, butter, milk powder, and salt, and mix well. Combine white flour with whole wheat flour and add to the yeast mixture, mixing well. Turn out on floured board and knead until smooth and elastic, about 10 minutes. Place in greased bowl and turn over so both sides of dough are greased. Cover bowl tightly with plastic wrap and set in a warm place to rise until double in bulk, about 1 hour.

Punch down, turn over, cover, and let rise again until almost double in bulk, about 30 minutes. Punch down, turn out on floured board, and divide dough into 8 equal parts. Form each piece into a smooth round ball. Place on greased baking sheets several inches apart. Press each ball to flatten. Cover and let rise in warm place until double in bulk, about 1 hour.

Meanwhile, preheat oven at 375°. Bake 10

CORN STICKS

vegetable shortening
2 eggs
1 cup milk
¼ cup melted butter or margarine
1 teaspoon grated onion
1½ cups cornmeal (preferably stone-
    ground cornmeal)
2 tablespoons brown sugar
3 teaspoons baking powder
¾ teaspoon salt

Preheat oven at 375°. Grease iron corn stick pans
eavy madeleine molds with vegetable shortening
put in oven. Beat eggs lightly. Add milk, melted
er, and onion, and beat again. Combine cornmeal,
r, baking powder, and salt, mixing well. Add dry
edients to liquid ingredients, mixing quickly, and
n into hot corn stick pans, filling just to top.
Bake 12–15 minutes, depending on size of sticks.
out on wire rack. These should be eaten shortly
they are made.
Makes 12 or more, depending on size of sticks in
mold.

DWICH SUGGESTION: Chili Scrambled Eggs in Corn
s

minutes. Brush with beaten egg and bake 7–10 minutes longer. Cool on wire rack. If not using within a few hours, wrap tightly in plastic wrap or aluminum foil to store.

Makes 8.

SANDWICH SUGGESTIONS: Hammy Herb-Mustard Hamburgers, Trailside Sandwiches, Tuna Totes

CRUMPETS

Unless you own some crumpet rings, you'll need to do a little advance preparation in order to make crumpets. Save 3 or 4 tuna fish cans (6½ ounce size) or small pineapple cans from which you have neatly removed the tops and bottoms, as well as the labels, washed thoroughly, and dried. You can use them in place of crumpet rings. Or you can use 3-inch or 4-inch flan rings or poaching rings if you happen to have them. Unlike English muffins, you don't split crumpets before eating them. You butter them on the top side, which is holey and absorbs butter thirstily.

> **1 package active dry yeast**
> **¾ cup warm water, about 115°**
> **½ teaspoon sugar**
> **¾ cup warm milk, about 115°**
> **2 cups white flour**
> **½ teaspoon salt**

Sprinkle yeast over ¼ cup of the warm water. Add the sugar and stir until yeast is dissolved. Set in a warm place until mixture begins to become foamy, about 5 minutes. Add balance of warm water and warm milk.

Sift flour and salt together into a bowl. Make a well in the center and pour the yeast mixture into the hole. With a wooden spoon gradually mix in all the flour and beat to a smooth thick batter. Cover and set in a warm place 30–45 minutes.

Grease 3 or 4 metal rings and an iron griddle or large iron skillet. Set the rings on the griddle, spacing apart evenly. Heat the griddle and rings until quite warm. It is not necessary to stir down the batter. Pour

the batter into the rings to a depth and smooth out to edges of the r spatula. Cook slowly over low he or until bubbles that appear on the off rings, turn the crumpets, and minutes. Regrease griddle and rin continue to make remaining crum ready to use.

To serve, toast the crumpets toasting bottom well and top light bubbled side) of crumpets well with

Makes 14 or more, dependir used.

SANDWICH SUGGESTIONS: Arnold Crabs on Crumpets, Orange and Canadi fins

or h
and
butt
suga
ingr
spoo

Turr
afte

you

SAN
Stick

CHAPPATI

1 cup whole wheat flour
pinch of salt
½ cup (approximately) water

Place flour in bowl and combine with salt. Add enough water to make a fairly stiff dough. Knead on floured board about 5 minutes. Return to bowl, cover with plastic wrap or a plate, and allow to rest about 1 hour.

Knead again lightly. Divide into 5 or 6 equal parts. Form each into a ball. Flour each ball and roll out as thin as possible on floured board with floured rolling pin.

Heat a dry cast-iron griddle or heavy skillet over medium heat. Toast chappati, one at a time, on the dry heated griddle until they blister on one side. Turn and toast the other side. It will take about 2 minutes on each side. Regulate flame if necessary so chappati do not scorch.

Chappati can be left flat or folded over before being removed from heat. If desired, butter before eating, or use as directed in individual recipe.

Makes 5 or 6.

SANDWICH SUGGESTIONS: Chappati with Eggplant Tahini; Chappati with Tomato, Cheese, and Sprouts

WHEAT GERM BREAD

1 package active dry yeast
1⅓ cups warm water, about 115°
2 tablespoons brown sugar
1½ tablespoons vegetable oil
2¾ or more cups white flour
½ cup whole wheat flour
¼ cup wheat germ
¼ cup instant nonfat dry milk powder
1 teaspoon salt
milk

Sprinkle yeast over ⅓ cup of the warm water in a large bowl and stir until yeast is dissolved. Add 1 teaspoon of the brown sugar and stir until dissolved. Set in a warm place until mixture begins to become foamy, about 5 minutes. Add balance of warm water and brown sugar, and the vegetable oil. In a separate bowl combine white flour, whole wheat flour, wheat germ, milk powder, and salt, and add to yeast mixture, mixing well.

Turn out on floured board and knead 5–10 minutes until smooth and elastic, kneading in more white flour if necessary. Place in greased bowl, turn dough over to grease other side, cover bowl tightly with plastic wrap, and set in a warm place to rise until double in bulk.

Punch down, knead lightly, and shape into loaf. Place in a greased 5″ x 9″ loaf pan, cover with plastic wrap, and set in warm place to rise again until double in bulk.

Meanwhile, preheat oven at 375° and bake 30 minutes. Brush with milk and bake 10 minutes longer,

or until loaf sounds hollow when tapped on the bottom. Remove from pan and cool on wire rack. Do not
slice until completely cool. Wrap tightly in aluminum
foil or plastic wrap to store.

Makes 1 loaf.

SANDWICH SUGGESTIONS: Beety Beef Fries, Potato Chip
Crunch Sandwich, Sausage Sandwich with Sautéed Apple Slices,
Stars and Stripes

FOUR GRAIN BREAD

1 cup skim milk

¾ cup water

1 cup cornmeal (preferably stone-ground
    cornmeal)

½ stick butter or margarine

½ cup warm water, about 115°

2 packages active dry yeast

2 tablespoons sugar

⅓ cup unsulphured molasses

1 tablespoon salt

½ cup buckwheat flour

½ cup pure wheat bran (not bran cereal)

¼ cup wheat germ

1 cup whole wheat flour

3 cups (approximately) white flour

Combine skim milk and water in saucepan and bring to boil. Put cornmeal in a large bowl and add the hot liquid gradually, stirring well so that no lumps form. Add butter and stir until melted. Allow to sit 10 minutes, stirring occasionally.

Meanwhile, put warm water in a small bowl. Sprinkle yeast over water, add 1 teaspoon of the sugar, and stir until yeast is dissolved. Set in a warm place about 5 minutes until mixture starts to become foamy. Add remaining sugar, molasses, and salt to the cornmeal mixture. Add the yeast mixture to cornmeal mixture. Add buckwheat flour, bran, wheat germ, and whole wheat flour and mix well. Add 2 cups white flour, one at a time, mixing well. Turn out on floured board and knead about 7 minutes until smooth and elastic, kneading in about 1 more cup of white flour.

Place in greased bowl, turn over so dough is greased on both sides, cover bowl tightly with plastic wrap, and set in warm place to rise until double in bulk.

Punch down, and allow to rest 10 minutes. Turn out on floured board and cut dough in half. Shape into 2 loaves. Place in 2 greased 8½″ x 4½″ loaf pans. Cover with plastic wrap and let rise in a warm place until double in bulk.

Meanwhile, preheat oven at 375°. Bake about 40 minutes, or until loaves sound hollow when tapped on the bottom. Remove from pans and cool on wire rack. Do not slice until completely cool. Wrap tightly in aluminum foil or plastic wrap to store.

Makes 2 loaves.

SANDWICH SUGGESTIONS: Beety Beef Fries, Sausage Sandwich with Sautéed Apple Slices, Tangy Crab-Shrimp Sandwich (Grilled Sandwich No. 4)

SOUTHERN POTATO BREAD

1 medium-size potato
¼ cup vegetable oil
¼ cup plus 1 teaspoon sugar
1 teaspoon salt
1 package active dry yeast
¼ cup warm water, about 115°
1 egg
⅓ cup milk
3¼ (or more) cups white flour
vegetable oil
melted butter or margarine

Peel the potato, cut in chunks, and boil until soft. Reserve potato water. Mash the potato in a bowl and add ½ cup of the potato water. Add vegetable oil, ¼ cup sugar, and salt, and mix well.

Sprinkle yeast over the warm water and stir until dissolved. Add remaining teaspoon sugar and stir until dissolved. Set in a warm place until mixture begins to become foamy, about 5 minutes. Add to the potato mixture. Beat egg lightly and combine with milk. Add to potato mixture.

Place flour in a large bowl. Add the potato mixture and blend well to make a soft dough. Turn out on floured board and knead until smooth and elastic, about 10 minutes, kneading in more flour if necessary. Place in greased bowl and turn dough over so both sides are greased. Cover bowl tightly with plastic wrap and set in warm place to rise until double in bulk.

Punch down with floured hand and knead lightly on floured board. Shape into loaf and place in greased 5" x 9" loaf pan. Brush top with vegetable oil. Cover with plastic wrap and set in warm place to rise until double in bulk.

Preheat oven at 400° and bake for 20 minutes. Reduce temperature to 300° and bake 25 minutes longer without opening oven door. Remove from oven and tap to see if bottom of bread sounds hollow. If not, return to oven for 10 minutes longer. Turn out on wire rack to cool. Brush top with melted butter. Do not slice until completely cool. Wrap tightly in aluminum foil or plastic wrap to store.

Makes 1 loaf.

SANDWICH SUGGESTIONS: Any sandwich calling for firm white bread

CHALLAH

1 package active dry yeast
¾ cup warm water, about 115°
2 teaspoons sugar
3 cups white flour
1 teaspoon salt
2 eggs
2 tablespoons vegetable oil
1 egg yolk
1 tablespoon water
poppy seeds

Sprinkle yeast over ¼ cup of the warm water in a small bowl and stir until dissolved. Add sugar and stir again. Set in a warm place until mixture starts to become foamy, about 5 minutes.

Combine flour and salt in a bowl. Beat the eggs lightly in another bowl and stir in the vegetable oil and remaining warm water. Stir the yeast mixture into the egg mixture. Add to the flour and mix well. Turn out on floured board and knead 5–10 minutes until smooth and elastic. Place dough in greased bowl and turn dough over so both sides are greased. Cover bowl tightly with plastic wrap and set in a warm place until double in bulk, about 1 hour.

Punch down, reshape into a ball, and roll around in bowl until again greased all over. Recover and let rise again until double in bulk, about 45 minutes.

Punch down and turn out on floured board. Knead lightly for a few seconds. Divide into 3 equal parts and form each into a sausage shape about 15 inches long, by rolling back and forth on the board and pulling and stretching. Pinch the 3 pieces together at one end and braid. Pinch other end together. Turn both ends under. Lift braided loaf and place in greased 5" x 9" loaf pan. Cover and allow to rise again in warm place until double in bulk.

Meanwhile, preheat oven at 375°. Beat the egg yolk slightly and stir in the tablespoon of water. Brush top of bread all over with the egg yolk mixture. Sprinkle liberally with poppy seeds. Bake about 45 minutes or until nicely browned; loaf should sound hollow when tapped on bottom. Remove from pan and cool on wire rack. Do not slice until completely cool. Wrap tightly in aluminum foil or plastic wrap to store, but it is preferable to eat this bread the day it is made.

Makes 1 loaf.

SANDWICH SUGGESTION: French-toasted Challah Sandwich with Tart Cherries and Cream Cheese

SAFFRON BREAD

⅛ teaspoon saffron
1 tablespoon warm water
1 cup milk, scalded
¼ cup sugar
½ stick butter or margarine, softened
1 package active dry yeast
1 egg, beaten
1 teaspoon salt
generous pinch of mace
4 cups (approximately) white flour
⅓ cup currants
melted butter or margarine

Stir saffron into warm water and set aside. Put milk in large bowl and add sugar and softened butter, stirring until butter is melted, or nearly melted. Add saffron water. Sprinkle yeast over mixture and stir until yeast is dissolved. Set in a warm place about 10 minutes, until mixture starts to become foamy. Add egg, salt, and mace, and mix well. Add 3 cups of flour and mix well. Add currants and mix well. Add enough flour (about 1 cup) to make a fairly stiff dough. Knead about 10 minutes on floured board. Place in greased bowl and turn dough over to grease other side. Cover bowl tightly with plastic wrap and set in a warm place to rise until double in bulk.

Punch down. Turn out onto floured board and knead lightly. Form into a loaf and place in greased 5" x 9" loaf pan. Brush with melted butter. Cover loosely with plastic wrap and set in warm place to rise again until double in bulk. Bread should puff well up over the top of the pan.

Meanwhile, preheat oven at 400°. Bake about 40 minutes or until loaf sounds hollow when tapped on bottom. Remove from pan and cool on wire rack. Do not slice until completely cool. Wrap tightly in aluminum foil or plastic wrap to store.

Makes 1 loaf.

SANDWICH SUGGESTION: Saffron Toast Cottage Cheese Sandwich

IRISH SEEDY BREAD

1 egg
1½ cups (approximately) buttermilk
4 cups sifted white flour
1 teaspoon baking soda
1 teaspoon salt
1 tablespoon sugar
1 tablespoon caraway seed

Preheat oven at 425°. Beat egg lightly and combine with 1 cup buttermilk. Sift flour, baking soda, salt, and sugar together into a bowl. Add caraway seeds and toss well. Make a well in the center and pour egg-buttermilk mixture in. Mix in quickly, and add about ½ cup more buttermilk, or enough to make a soft dough. Turn out on floured board and knead lightly for a few seconds. Shape into a ball, flatten slightly, and set in the center of a greased 8-inch round cake pan. With a sharp wet knife cut a deep cross on the top and across and down the sides, making the cuts shallower on the sides.

Bake about 35 minutes, or until loaf sounds hollow when tapped on the bottom. Remove from pan and cool on wire rack. Do not slice until completely cool. Wrap tightly in aluminum foil or plastic wrap to store. This bread is at its best when sliced and toasted.

Makes 1 loaf.

SANDWICH SUGGESTIONS: Fruitarian Sandwiches, Irish Seedy Bread Bacon Sandwich

HERB BREAD

¾ cup milk
2 tablespoons butter or margarine
¼ cup warm water, about 115°
1 package active dry yeast
2 tablespoons brown sugar
1 teaspoon salt
1 egg
1 teaspoon sage
1 teaspoon bruised caraway seed (use back
    of a spoon, or mortar and pestle)
2 tablespoons very finely chopped parsley
¼ teaspoon nutmeg
3 cups white flour
¼ cup wheat germ
1 egg yolk mixed with 1 tablespoon milk

Scald milk. Remove from stove, add butter, and stir until melted. Cool until lukewarm.

Meanwhile, put warm water in a large bowl and sprinkle the yeast over it. Add 1 teaspoon of the sugar and stir until yeast is dissolved. Set in a warm place until mixture starts to become foamy, about 5 minutes. Add milk mixture to yeast mixture, along with remaining sugar and salt. Beat egg lightly and add along with sage, caraway seed, parsley, and nutmeg. Add flour and wheat germ and mix well.

Turn out on floured board and knead about 10 minutes until smooth and elastic. Place in greased bowl and turn dough over so both sides are greased. Cover bowl tightly with plastic wrap and allow to rise in warm place until double in bulk. Punch down and knead lightly on floured board. Shape into a loaf and place in well-greased 5" x 9" loaf pan. Cover and allow to rise again in warm place until double in bulk.

Meanwhile, preheat oven at 350°. Brush top of bread with egg yolk–milk mixture. Bake 30–40 minutes, or until loaf sounds hollow when tapped on the bottom. Remove from pan and cool on wire rack. Do not slice until completely cool. Wrap tightly in aluminum foil or plastic wrap to store.

Makes 1 loaf.

SANDWICH SUGGESTIONS: Cheddar–Green Pepper–Garlic Sandwich (Grilled Sandwich No. 1), Nutty Seedy Sandwich, Souffléed Cheddar Sandwich

CHEDDAR BREAD

1¾ cups milk
¼ cup vegetable oil
1 package active dry yeast
¼ cup warm water, about 115°
¼ cup sugar
4 cups (approximately) white flour
¼ cup wheat germ
2 teaspoons salt
1 teaspoon dry mustard
½ pound sharp Cheddar, shredded
milk

Scald the milk. Remove from stove and add vegetable oil. Allow to cool to lukewarm. Meanwhile, add the yeast to the warm water, stirring until dissolved. Add ¼ teaspoon of the sugar to the yeast and stir again. Set in a warm place until mixture starts to become foamy, about 5 minutes. Combine milk mixture and yeast mixture.

In another bowl combine 2 cups of the flour, wheat germ, the remaining sugar, salt, and mustard, mixing well. Add to yeast mixture and combine well. Toss the Cheddar with remaining 2 cups of flour and add to yeast mixture, combining well. Turn out on floured board and knead 10 minutes, kneading in more flour if dough is too soft, until smooth and elastic. Place in greased bowl, turn dough over to grease other side, cover bowl tightly with plastic wrap, and set in a warm place to rise until double in bulk.

Punch down, knead lightly, and divide dough into 2 equal parts. Shape into 2 loaves and set in two 4½" x 8" loaf pans. Cover lightly and set in warm place to rise again until double in bulk.

Meanwhile, preheat oven at 350°. Bake about 25 minutes, brush tops with milk, and continue baking about 10 minutes longer, or until loaves sound hollow when tapped on the bottom. Cool on wire rack. Do not slice until completely cool. Wrap tightly in aluminum foil or plastic wrap to store. This bread is at its best when sliced and toasted.

Makes 2 loaves.

SANDWICH SUGGESTIONS: Ham-Mushroom Sandwich (Grilled Sandwich No. 5), Holy Mackerel Sandwich

TOMATO BREAD

¼ cup warm water, about 115°
1 package active dry yeast
2 tablespoons honey
2 tablespoons vegetable oil
¾ cup tomato sauce
1 teaspoon salt
¼ teaspoon oregano
1 teaspoon basil
1 teaspoon dill seed
2½–3 cups whole wheat flour
melted butter or margarine

Put water in a large bowl and sprinkle the yeast over it, along with 1 teaspoon of the honey. Stir until yeast is dissolved. Set in a warm place until mixture starts to become foamy, 5–10 minutes. Add remaining honey, oil, tomato sauce, salt, oregano, basil, dill seed, and 2½ cups of whole wheat flour. Combine well and add more flour if necessary to make a fairly firm dough. Turn out on whole-wheat-floured board and knead 5–10 minutes until smooth and elastic. Place in greased bowl and turn dough over so that both sides are greased. Cover bowl tightly with plastic wrap and allow to rise in warm place until double in bulk.

Punch down. Knead lightly on floured board. Shape into a round loaf. Place on an 8-inch greased cake pan. Brush with melted butter. Cover with plastic wrap and let rise again in warm place until double in bulk.

Meanwhile, preheat oven at 350°. Bake 45–50 minutes, or until loaf sounds hollow when tapped on bottom. Remove from pan and cool on wire rack. Do not slice until completely cool. Wrap tightly in aluminum foil or plastic wrap to store.

Makes 1 loaf.

SANDWICH SUGGESTIONS: Lashing Tongue Sandwich, Nutted Tuna and Spinach Sandwich, Smoked Turkey Breast on Tomato Bread

DILL BREAD

1 package active dry yeast
¼ cup warm water, about 115°
1 tablespoon sugar
1 cup creamed cottage cheese
1 egg, lightly beaten
2 tablespoons grated onion
1 tablespoon melted butter or margarine
1 tablespoon dill seed
1 teaspoon salt
¼ teaspoon baking soda
2 cups white flour
¼ cup wheat germ
milk
coarse salt

Sprinkle yeast over warm water, add ½ teaspoon of the sugar, and stir until yeast is dissolved. Set in a warm place until mixture starts to become foamy, about 5 minutes.

Meanwhile, heat the cottage cheese in a saucepan until lukewarm. Put in a bowl and combine with yeast mixture. Add the egg, onion, butter, remaining sugar, dill seed, salt, and baking soda. Combine flour and wheat germ and add to dough gradually, mixing until well blended. Place in greased bowl and turn over so dough is greased on both sides. Cover bowl tightly with plastic wrap and allow to rise in warm place until double in bulk.

Stir down and knead lightly for a minute. Turn into greased 1½-quart casserole. Cover and let rise 30–40 minutes.

Meanwhile, preheat oven at 350°. Bake 40–50 minutes, or until loaf sounds hollow when tapped on the bottom. Before last 10 minutes of baking, brush top with milk and sprinkle with coarse salt. Turn out on wire rack. This can be sliced hot or cold. Wrap tightly in aluminum foil or plastic wrap to store.

Makes 1 loaf.

SANDWICH SUGGESTIONS: Nutted Tuna and Spinach Sandwich, Towering Eggplant Sandwich

OATMEAL BREAD

½ cup milk
¼ cup butter or margarine
2 tablespoons unsulphured molasses
1 package active dry yeast
¼ cup warm water, about 115°
2 tablespoons brown sugar
1 egg, lightly beaten
2¼ (or more) cups white flour
1 cup rolled oats
1 teaspoon salt

Combine milk, butter, and molasses in a small saucepan and heat, stirring, until butter has melted. Set aside to cool to lukewarm.

Meanwhile, sprinkle yeast over warm water. Add 1 teaspoon of the sugar and stir until yeast is dissolved. Set in a warm place until mixture starts to become foamy, about 5 minutes. Combine molasses mixture and yeast mixture. Stir in the beaten egg and remaining sugar. Toss flour, rolled oats, and salt together and add to yeast mixture gradually, mixing well. Turn out on floured board and knead about 10 minutes until smooth and elastic, kneading in more flour if necessary. Dough should be fairly soft. Place in greased bowl, turn dough over so both sides are greased, and cover bowl tightly with plastic wrap. Set in a warm place to rise until double in bulk.

Punch down. Knead lightly a few seconds and shape into loaf. Place in greased 8½″ x 4½″ loaf pan. Brush with water and sprinkle additional rolled oats over top. Cover and set in warm place again to rise until double in bulk.

Meanwhile, preheat oven at 350°. Bake 40–45 minutes or until loaf sounds hollow when tapped on bottom. Cool on wire rack. Do not slice until completely cool. Wrap tightly in aluminum foil or plastic wrap to store.

Makes 1 loaf.

SANDWICH SUGGESTIONS: Chicken Divan Sandwich, Eggplant Baconwich, Walnutwiches

SWEDISH LYMPA BREAD

1 teaspoon anise seed
1 teaspoon fennel seed
1 package active dry yeast
¼ cup warm water, about 115°
1 teaspoon sugar
½ cup milk
1 tablespoon butter or margarine
3 tablespoons molasses
2 tablespoons grated orange peel
½ teaspoon salt
1 egg, slightly beaten
1¼ cups rye flour
1¼–1½ cups white flour

Crush anise seed and fennel seed with a hammer or mortar and pestle. Combine seeds. Sprinkle yeast over warm water and stir until yeast is dissolved. Stir in sugar. Set in a warm place until mixture starts to become foamy, about 5 minutes.

Meanwhile, scald milk and pour into a bowl. Add butter and stir until melted. Add molasses, orange peel, salt, and the combined seeds. Add beaten egg and mix well. Add yeast mixture. Add rye flour and mix until smooth. Add enough of the white flour to make a dough slightly firm but not stiff. Turn out on floured board and knead until smooth and elastic, about 10 minutes. Place in greased bowl and turn dough over so both sides are greased. Cover bowl tightly with plastic wrap and set in a warm place to rise until double in bulk, about 1½ hours.

Punch down and knead lightly. Shape into an oval loaf. Place on greased baking sheet, cover, and let rise again in warm place until double in bulk, about 35–40 minutes.

Meanwhile, preheat oven at 375°. Bake 30–35 minutes, or until loaf sounds hollow when tapped on bottom. Turn out of pan and cool on wire rack. Cool completely before slicing. Wrap tightly in aluminum foil or plastic wrap to store.

Makes 1 loaf.

SANDWICH SUGGESTIONS: Garden Cucumber Sandwiches, Grilled Chutney Cheese Sandwich, Souffléed Cheddar Sandwich

SCANDINAVIAN PUMPERNICKEL

½ cup plus 1 tablespoon unsulphured
    molasses (such as "Grandma's" brand.
    Do not use very dark molasses such as
    Barbados or blackstrap.)
1 tablespoon grated orange peel
1½ teaspoons salt
2 tablespoons caraway seed
2 cups cold buttermilk
1 package active dry yeast
¼ cup warm water, about 115°
¼ teaspoon sugar
3 cups rye flour
3 cups (approximately) white flour
¼ cup cold water

Combine ½ cup molasses, orange peel, salt, and
caraway seed in small saucepan and bring to boil, stirring. Remove from heat and pour into large bowl. Add
buttermilk and mix well. Sprinkle yeast over warm
water, add sugar, and stir until yeast is dissolved. Set
in a warm place until mixture starts to become foamy,
about 5 minutes. Add to the buttermilk mixture which
should now be lukewarm. Stir in the rye flour gradually, mixing well. Add white flour and mix well. Allow
to stand 15 minutes undisturbed.

Turn out on floured board (using white flour for
the board) and knead about 10 minutes until smooth
and elastic, kneading in more white flour if necessary.
Place in greased bowl and turn dough over to grease
other side. Cover bowl tightly with plastic wrap and
set in a warm place to rise until double in bulk.

Punch down, knead lightly, and divide dough into

2 equal parts. Shape each into an oval loaf about 8 inches long. Set well apart on a greased baking sheet, cover lightly with plastic wrap, and allow to rise until nearly double in bulk.

Meanwhile, preheat oven at 350°. Combine remaining molasses with cold water. Brush the loaves with this mixture, bake 15 minutes, brush again, and bake another 15 minutes. Brush again and continue baking another 15–20 minutes, or until loaves sound hollow when tapped on bottom. (Total baking time is 45–50 minutes.) Brush again with mixture. Remove from oven and set loaves on wire rack to cool. Do not slice until completely cool. Wrap tightly in aluminum foil or plastic wrap to store.

Makes 2 loaves.

SANDWICH SUGGESTIONS: Blue Cheese–Turkey–Salami Sandwich (Grilled Sandwich No. 3), Dansk Smørrebrød (Danish Open-faced Sandwiches): Smoked Eel and Danish Cheese (Danish Sandwich No. 3), Herring Tidbits or Anchovies and Hard-cooked Egg Slices (Danish Sandwich No. 5), German Liverwurst Caprice, Stars and Stripes

DANISH RYE BREAD

½ cup warm water, about 115°
2 packages active dry yeast
1 teaspoon sugar
1½ teaspoons salt
2 tablespoons caraway seed
1 tablespoon melted butter or margarine
6 cups rye flour
2 cups white flour
3 cups buttermilk
melted butter or margarine

Put water in a large bowl and sprinkle the yeast over it. Add sugar and stir until yeast is dissolved. Set in a warm place until mixture starts to become foamy, about 5 minutes. Add salt, caraway seed, and 1 tablespoon melted butter. Sift rye flour and white flour together and add alternately with buttermilk. Mix well and turn out on floured board. Knead about 10 minutes until smooth and elastic. Place in greased bowl and turn dough over so both sides are greased. Cover bowl tightly with plastic wrap and allow to rise in warm place until double in bulk, 1½–2½ hours.

Punch down. Turn out on floured board and knead lightly. Cut dough into 2 equal parts. Shape into loaves and place in two 5″ x 9″ greased loaf pans. Cover and allow to rise again in warm place until double in bulk.

Meanwhile, preheat oven at 400°. Brush tops of loaves with melted butter and bake 45–50 minutes or until loaves sound hollow when tapped on bottom. Remove from pans and cool on wire rack. Do not slice until completely cool. Wrap tightly in aluminum foil or plastic wrap to store.

   Makes 2 loaves.

SANDWICH SUGGESTIONS: Blue Cheese–Turkey–Salami (Grilled Sandwich No. 3), Crabmeat-Avocado Sandwich, Dansk Smørrebrød (Danish Open-faced Sandwiches): Liver Pâté (Danish Sandwich No. 2) Danish Salami with Jellied Consommé (Danish Sandwich No. 4), Ham with Hearts of Palm Béarnaise Sandwich, Roquefort Steak Sandwich, Sausage Sandwich with Sautéed Apple Slices

DARK SOY-CAROB BREAD

3 cups warm water, about 115°
1 package active dry yeast
¾ cup honey
½ cup vegetable oil
½ cup instant nonfat dry milk powder
½ cup sunflower seeds
1 cup wheat bran (not bran cereal)
1 cup soy flour (available at health-food stores)
1 cup carob powder (available at health-food stores)
5–6 cups whole wheat flour

Put warm water in a large bowl and sprinkle the yeast over it. Add honey and stir until yeast is dissolved. Set in a warm place until mixture starts to become foamy, about 5 minutes. Add oil and milk powder. Put sunflower seeds through blender or food processor until fine. Add to yeast mixture along with bran, soy flour, carob powder, and enough whole wheat flour to make a stiff dough. Turn out on floured board and knead until smooth and elastic, about 10 minutes. Place in greased bowl and turn dough over so both sides are greased. Cover bowl tightly with plastic wrap and allow to rise in warm place until double in bulk.

Punch down. Turn out on floured board and knead lightly. Cut dough into 2 equal parts. Shape into loaves and place in two 5" x 9" greased loaf pans. Cover and allow to rise again in warm place until double in bulk.

Meanwhile, preheat oven at 375°. Bake 45–55 minutes, or until loaves sound hollow when tapped on

Knead until smooth and elastic, about 15 minutes, kneading in more white flour if necessary. Place in greased bowl and turn dough over so both sides are greased. Cover bowl tightly with plastic wrap and allow to rise in warm place until double in bulk.

Punch down and turn out on lightly floured board. Cut dough into 2 equal parts. Shape into smooth balls. Place in 2 greased 8-inch round cake pans, and turn over so dough is greased on both sides. Cover and allow to rise again in warm place until double in bulk, about 45 minutes.

Meanwhile, preheat oven at 350°. Bake 40 minutes. Brush with milk and bake another 10 minutes, or until loaves sound hollow when tapped on bottom. Remove from pans and cool on wire rack. Do not slice until completely cool. Wrap tightly in aluminum foil or plastic wrap to store.

Makes 2 loaves.

SANDWICH SUGGESTIONS: Golden Tongue Sandwich, Greek Salad Sandwich, Muenster-Bacon-Scallion Sandwich (Grilled Sandwich No. 2), Stars and Stripes

WHOLE WHEAT ITALIAN BREAD

1 package active dry yeast
1 cup warm water, about 115°
¼ teaspoon sugar
1½ cups (or more) white flour
1 tablespoon vegetable oil
1½ teaspoons salt
1 cup whole wheat flour
cornmeal
1 egg white
1 tablespoon cold water

Sprinkle yeast over ¼ cup of the warm water in a large bowl and stir until yeast is dissolved. Add sugar, stir, and leave bowl in warm place until mixture starts to become foamy, about 5 minutes. Add balance of warm water, 1½ cups white flour, oil, and salt, and mix for several minutes. Add whole wheat flour and mix until smooth. If necessary, add a little more white flour if the dough seems too soft, but it should not be a firm dough. Turn out on floured board and knead about 10 minutes until smooth and elastic. Place dough in greased bowl and turn dough over so that both sides are greased. Cover bowl tightly with plastic wrap and set in a warm place to rise until more than double, and nearly triple, in bulk. This will take about 2½ hours.

Punch down and knead about 15 seconds. Re-grease the bowl and put the dough back in it. Turn dough over so both sides are greased. Re-cover with plastic wrap and set in warm place to rise again until more than double in bulk, about 1–1¼ hours.

Punch down and turn out on floured board. Fold over once. Pat out into an oval about 8" x 12". Fold in half lengthwise. Seal edges with fingers. Turn up so that seal is on top, and flatten into an oval. Press a trench down the length of the bread with the side of the hand. Fold in half lengthwise. Seal edges with fingers. Turn over so that seal is on the bottom. Sprinkle some flour on a clean dish towel and rub into the towel. Set the towel on a tray or baking sheet. Measure the baking sheet you will be using to bake the bread. If the bread is less than 2 inches shorter than the pan length, roll the bread back and forth between your palms to lengthen it a bit. If the bread is too long, lift and coax it into a shorter length. With the aid of a flat-edged tray or similar thin flat item, transfer the bread to the floured towel, seam side up. Place a rolling pin or similarly shaped object on either side of the bread under the towel to hold the loaf in shape while it rises. Cover the bread with another clean, floured dish towel. Cover the towel with plastic wrap to prevent drafts from getting to the bread. Leave in a warm place until nearly triple in bulk.

Meanwhile, preheat oven at 425°. Arrange one shelf on the lowest position in oven and one shelf near the upper third of oven. Set a pan containing about an inch of hot water on the bottom shelf. Sprinkle cornmeal over the baking sheet you will use for baking the bread. (An Italian bread pan is ideal.) Transfer the bread to the baking sheet or bread pan, seam side down. With a single-edge razor blade make three diagonal slashes in the top of the bread, less than ½ inch deep and about 2 inches apart. Beat the egg white lightly and add the cold water. Brush entire exposed surface of bread with the mixture. Bake 10 minutes and brush again. Reduce oven temperature to 350° and continue baking 20–30 minutes, or until loaf sounds hollow when tapped on bottom. Cool on wire rack. Do not slice until completely cool. Wrap in wax paper and use within 24 hours of baking. Alternately, wrap cooled bread tightly in plastic wrap and freeze immediately. Thaw when ready to use, and heat slightly in oven if desired.

Makes 1 loaf.

SANDWICH SUGGESTIONS: Boursin Omelet Bites, European Workmen's Sandwiches, Ricotta Caponata Canapé, Sole Sandwiches over Fennel Fire

BRIOCHE

Brioche must be started the day before you plan to bake it. The ideal time to begin making it is in mid-afternoon. Then you will have time to mix and work with it and allow it 4 hours to rise in a warm place before you refrigerate it overnight for a cool rising. Next day you shape it, allow it a final rising in its mold, and bake it. It is a truly magnificent bread that turns any snack time or brunch into a feast, and is worth the time and effort of making it.

> ¼ **cup milk**
> **1½ packages active dry yeast**
> **4 cups sifted white flour**
> **1 tablespoon sugar**
> **2 teaspoons salt**
> **6 eggs**
> **1 cup (2 sticks) sweet butter (no substitutes)**
> **softened butter for greasing mold**
> **1 egg, lightly beaten**

Heat milk to 115° and put in small bowl. Sprinkle yeast over milk and stir until yeast is dissolved. Add ½–¾ cup flour—enough so that the mixture holds together well. Knead on board for 2–3 minutes. Shape into a ball. Put back in bowl. Cover bowl with plastic wrap and allow to stand in warm place 30 minutes.

Meanwhile, put remaining flour in a bowl. Add sugar and salt and toss well to combine. Make a well in the center and put 4 of the eggs in it. With the fingers, work the flour mixture gradually into the eggs. Break the remaining eggs into a cup and add to the flour mixture gradually, again working in with the fingers. The dough will be soft and sticky. Work the dough in the bowl until it feels elastic.

Turn out onto floured board. Beat the dough on the board by picking it up and throwing it down on the board, using wrist motion to do the throwing. Throw down at least 125 times. Dough stretches out when thrown, so fold it over before throwing down again.

Put cold butter on a board and beat it with a rolling pin until softened, or, if you can work quickly with your hands, knead the butter with your hands until pliable but not melting.

Return the beaten dough to the bowl. Work the butter into the dough, putting in several small pieces of butter at a time and working them in gently with the fingertips in a squeezing, kneading motion. When all the butter has been incorporated into the dough, add the yeast mixture. Mix and knead in the bowl until thoroughly combined. Do not allow any streaks to remain. The dough will be slightly soft and sticky. Turn into a large, clean, floured bowl. Cover tightly with plastic wrap and set in a warm place for 4 hours.

Punch down. The dough will be very light. Turn dough over. Cover tightly with plastic wrap and refrigerate 8 hours or overnight. (It will not hurt to leave it refrigerated several hours more than 8 hours.)

Punch down dough as much as it has risen; it will not have doubled in bulk. Turn out on floured board and allow to stand for 20 minutes. Take enough of the dough to fill about ⅔ of a large brioche mold, charlotte mold (about 6 inches in diameter at top), or similar mold. Form that dough into a ball and set it in the generously buttered mold. Take another piece of dough, about ¼ the amount already in the mold, and form into a ball. Roll back and forth between palms to shape the ball into a teardrop shape. With 3 fingers held together, push a hole halfway or more down into the large ball of dough which is in the mold. Fit the teardrop-shaped ball into the hole, pointed end down. (Any leftover dough can be shaped and baked in small, individual brioche tins, or it can be shaped into one ball and baked in any buttered pan into which it will fit so that it fills the pan ⅔ full.)

Cover and set in a warm place to rise until dough is just even with top of mold, about 1½ hours.

Meanwhile, preheat oven at 425°. Brush top of brioche with beaten egg, making sure not to allow the egg to run into the space between the teardrop-shaped ball and the large ball of dough. With scissors make 4 or 5 distinct snips around the brioche (not the tear-drop), to aid in rising and to form a design on the dough. Bake 30 minutes and test with cake tester or sharp-pointed knife to see if center is done. If not, bake 15 minutes longer, or until cake tester inserted in center comes out dry. If top of brioche starts to become too dark during baking, cover with a loose tent of aluminum foil. Remove from pan and cool on wire rack.

Makes 1 large brioche and a few small ones, depending on size of mold used.

SANDWICH SUGGESTION: Béarnaise Omelet Stuffed Brioche Wedges

BANANA BREAD

⅓ cup butter or margarine
1 cup dark brown sugar, firmly packed
2 eggs
1 cup mashed banana (about 2 bananas)
1¾ cups whole wheat flour
2 teaspoons baking powder
¼ teaspoon baking soda
½ teaspoon salt
½ cup chopped walnuts
½ cup chopped pitted dates

Preheat oven at 350°. Cream butter and add sugar gradually, beating until fluffy. Add eggs, one at a time, and mix well. Add mashed banana and mix well. Sift dry ingredients together and mix into batter. Add nuts and dates and mix well. Turn into greased 5" x 9" loaf pan and bake 1 hour, or until cake tester inserted in center comes out clean. Remove from pan and cool on wire rack. Do not slice until completely cool. Wrap tightly in aluminum foil or plastic wrap to store.

Makes 1 loaf.

SANDWICH SUGGESTION: Peanut Butter Lemon Marmalade Banana Bread Sandwich

PUMPKIN BREAD

¾ cup honey
⅓ cup vegetable oil
2 eggs
1 cup canned pumpkin or very thick cooked
    fresh pumpkin purée
1½ cups whole wheat flour
¾ teaspoon salt
½ teaspoon baking soda
½ teaspoon baking powder
1½ teaspoons cinnamon
½ teaspoon nutmeg
¼ teaspoon ground cloves
½ cup shelled pumpkin seeds (pepitas)

Preheat oven at 325°. Combine honey and oil. Add eggs and beat with eggbeater. Add pumpkin and mix well. Sift dry ingredients together and add to pumpkin mixture. Add pumpkin seeds, mix well, and turn into greased 5" x 9" loaf pan.

Bake 1 hour, or until cake tester inserted in center comes out clean. Remove from pan and cool on wire rack. Do not slice until completely cool. Wrap tightly in aluminum foil or plastic wrap to store.

Makes 1 loaf.

SANDWICH SUGGESTION: Ginger Pumpkin Sandwich

ORANGE SUNFLOWER BREAD

1 egg
⅔ cup orange juice
2 tablespoons grated orange peel, firmly packed
3 tablespoons melted butter or margarine
2 cups white flour
¾ cup sugar
1 teaspoon baking powder
½ teaspoon baking soda
½ teaspoon salt
¾ cup sunflower seeds

Preheat oven at 350°. Beat the egg and stir in orange juice and peel, mixing well. Add butter and mix well. Sift flour, sugar, baking powder, baking soda, and salt together into a large bowl. Add the egg mixture and combine well. Add sunflower seeds and mix thoroughly.

Turn mixture into well-greased 5" x 9" loaf pan. Bake about 1 hour, or until cake tester inserted in center comes out clean. Set the pan on a wire rack to cool for 10 minutes. Turn out bread onto wire rack and allow to cool completely before slicing. Wrap tightly in aluminum foil or plastic wrap to store.

Makes 1 loaf.

SANDWICH SUGGESTION: Vitamin C Sandwich

PECAN BREAD

1 egg
1 cup milk
3 cups sifted white flour
¾ cup sugar
½ teaspoon salt
3 teaspoons double-acting baking powder
3 tablespoons melted butter or margarine
½ cup ground pecans
½ cup chopped pecans

Beat egg lightly. Add milk and beat again. Sift flour, sugar, salt, and baking powder together into a bowl and add the egg-milk mixture. Add butter and pecans and mix thoroughly. Allow to stand 30 minutes.

Meanwhile, preheat oven at 300°. Turn batter into greased 5" x 9" loaf pan and bake 1¼–1½ hours, or until cake tester inserted in center comes out clean. Remove from pan and cool on wire rack. Do not slice until completely cool. Wrap tightly in plastic wrap or aluminum foil to store. This bread is best if baked the day before you plan to use it.

Makes 1 loaf.

SANDWICH SUGGESTION: Zippy Edam Sandwich

APPLE HONEY DATE BREAD

1½ cups pitted cut-up dates, loosely packed
¼ cup apple juice or cider
3 tablespoons butter or margarine
⅓ cup honey
¼ cup unsulphured molasses
1 egg, beaten
2 cups white flour
½ teaspoon salt
1½ teaspoons baking powder
½ teaspoon ginger
¼ teaspoon cinnamon
½ cup wheat germ
½ cup sour cream
1¼ cups finely chopped tart apple (peeled)
½ cup chopped walnuts

Preheat oven at 350°. Put dates in a small bowl and toss with apple juice. Set aside. Cream butter, add honey, and cream again. Add molasses and mix well. Add beaten egg and mix well. Sift flour, salt, baking powder, ginger, and cinnamon together into a bowl. Add wheat germ to flour mixture. Add flour mixture to butter mixture alternately with sour cream. Add apple, walnuts, and date–apple juice mixture. Turn into greased 5" x 9" loaf pan and smooth top with rubber spatula. Bake about 1½ hours, or until cake tester inserted in center comes out clean. Cool on wire rack. When completely cool wrap in aluminum foil or plastic wrap. Allow to mellow 8 hours or overnight before slicing. Makes 1 loaf.

SANDWICH SUGGESTIONS: Apple-Date-Chestnut Sandwich, Cashew Butter

SANDWICH BUTTERS
(Including Herb Butters)

Many sandwiches, particularly those with very simple fillings, such as roast beef, chicken, cheese, or egg, can be made outstanding by spreading the bread or toast with a good-tasting sandwich butter.

To make, cream 1 stick butter or margarine and add the ingredients listed to make the following butters:

Roquefort: 4 tablespoons crumbled Roquefort cheese
Parmesan: 4 tablespoons grated Parmesan cheese
Anchovy: 1 tablespoon anchovy paste, 1 teaspoon lemon juice, and ½ teaspoon paprika
Olive: 2 tablespoons finely chopped green or black olives, 2 teaspoons lemon juice, 1 teaspoon fine dry breadcrumbs
Horseradish: 3 tablespoons grated horseradish
Garlic: 1 clove mashed or finely minced garlic
Chive: 2 tablespoons snipped chives and 1 teaspoon lemon juice
Mustard: 2 tablespoons Dijon mustard or any preferred prepared mustard, or 2 teaspoons dry mustard
Spicy: 3 tablespoons ketchup, 1 teaspoon Worcestershire sauce, and Tabasco sauce to taste
Lemon: 1 teaspoon grated zest of lemon peel, 2 teaspoons lemon juice, and 1 teaspoon fine dry breadcrumbs
Egg yolk–lemon: yolks of 3 hard-cooked eggs put through ricer or fine sieve, 2 teaspoons lemon juice, salt, freshly ground pepper and Tabasco sauce to taste, and 1 teaspoon fine dry breadcrumbs
Nut: 4 tablespoons ground or minced walnuts, pecans,

cashews, almonds, or pistachios, and salt to taste

Pickle-pimiento: 4 tablespoons chopped pimiento, 2 tablespoons finely chopped flavorful pickles, 1 teaspoon fine dry breadcrumbs

Rémoulade: 2 tablespoons mayonnaise, 1 tablespoon chopped capers, 1 tablespoon snipped chives, 1 tablespoon chopped parsley, 1 tablespoon fresh chervil or 1 teaspoon dried chervil, 1 tablespoon fresh tarragon or 1 teaspoon dried tarragon, salt and freshly ground pepper to taste

Mint: 1 tablespoon chopped fresh mint (good on pita bread sandwiches)

Mixed herb: ½ teaspoon each fresh chopped rosemary, basil, and thyme, or ¼ teaspoon dried rosemary, ¼ teaspoon dried basil, and a generous pinch of thyme

Parsley: 3 tablespoons finely chopped parsley, 2 teaspoons lemon juice, and 1 teaspoon fine dry breadcrumbs

Tarragon, basil, oregano, marjoram, dill, rosemary, or **sage:** selecting one herb, use 1–2 tablespoons finely chopped fresh herb, or 1 teaspoon of the same dried herb, and a dash of lemon juice

Any of the above butters will keep several days in the refrigerator in small tightly sealed glass jars.

CLARIFIED BUTTER

Clarified butter is simple and quick to make, and has the advantage over regular butter of not burning when used for sautéing sandwiches and other foods. It also has better keeping qualities than unclarified butter, and can be kept in a small tightly sealed jar in the refrigerator.

1 stick (or more) butter (not margarine)

Melt butter in a small saucepan or in the top of a double boiler over hot water. Do not allow it to brown. Remove from heat (if using double boiler, remove lower part of double boiler). Allow to stand about 5 minutes. With a spoon skim off any skin that forms on top. Pour off the clear butter, which is the clarified butter, and discard the milky sediment at the bottom of the pan.

ABOUT MUSTARD

While a few people still plaster it on themselves to relieve chest colds, most people prefer to plaster mustard on their sandwiches. And well they might, for what can make a sandwich as tangy or tempting as a good mustard? Americans love mustard, and each year import millions of jars of prepared mustards from Europe and millions of tons of mustard seed from Canada for conversion into various kinds of prepared American mustards. There are many kinds to choose from, and a look at your supermarket or specialty food store condiment shelf will reveal a selection vast enough to please the most discriminating mustard connoisseur or just plain mustard freak. Some of the mustards are discussed below.

It's worth pointing out that we probably are in debt to the Romans for some of the best mustards we have today, since those people introduced the mustard seed into ancient Gaul. There it has been grown and processed into mustard for centuries. Burgundy, whose capital is Dijon, proved to be best suited to producing the fragrant condiment, and Dijon remains the largest and most famous mustard center of the world.

What makes Dijon mustard different from other mustards and gives it its enticing tart quality is verjuice, an acid juice extracted from unripened grapes. Other ingredients and method of preparation in the complex formula of Dijon mustard also contribute to the taste and texture of the finished product. Dijon mustard ranges from mild to extra strong (see labels), but even the extra-strong has none of the bite or tear-producing properties of, say, a hot Chinese mustard. There are also some nice herb mustards from Dijon, and you might look particularly for those flavored with tarragon or mixed Provençal herbs. Another French mustard, Bordeaux, a sweet-sour type, uses must from wine vats to lend it distinction.

Meaux, a town east and slightly north of Paris, which produces the best Brie in France, also produces one of the country's finest mustards, Pommery mustard, or Moutarde de Meaux, a lovely grainy and aromatic mustard. The famed gourmet of bygone years, Brillat-Savarin, said of it, "If it isn't Meaux, it isn't mustard." This may be something of an exaggeration or prejudice, but Meaux is a marvelous mustard and comes in a sturdy stone crock that is very much in keeping with its character. Savora mustard—smooth-textured, slightly sweet, yet tasty—is another French mustard that is very nice in sandwiches.

Düsseldorf is the best known of the German mustards, and the easiest to find in this country. It is mildly spiced and smooth in texture. A variety of other German mustards can be found in stores which specialize in German products, but none is as widely available as Düsseldorf.

For those who like a little punch to their mustard, English powdered mustard, which is somehow synonymous with the name Colman's, is the best bet. This dry mustard is the same type as that used by the Chinese for their hot mustard, and is ground from both black and light mustard seed; the black seed gives it its special fiery character. This is the mustard you mix with water in the quantity required for each use, and there is nothing subtle in its flavor. Although, oddly, the ingredients are not listed on the can, the powder is reputed to be made up solely of ground mustard seed and flour, with no vinegar, wine, salt, spices, or other ingredients to tone it down.

Most American mustards are made solely from light mustard seed, which gives them a mild, rather bland flavor preferred by many. Grey-Poupon mustard, which is an American version of the Grey-Poupon mustard of Dijon (and the Grey here is a name, not a color), is a pleasant mild mustard useful to have on hand and readily available in supermarkets. One distinct American mustard is Zatarain's Creole mustard from New Orleans. A nice grainy texture and mild spicy flavor make it very agreeable as a sandwich companion.

4. SANDWICHES FOR LUNCH TIME

Endless noon-day, glorious noon-day.
—JAMES MASON NEALE, translator, "Light's Abode, Celestial Salem," *from the Latin "Hierusalem Luminosa"*

What would lunch time be without sandwiches? Impossible to imagine, inconvenient, possibly dull, and not very satisfying as a steady diet. Every schoolchild, wage earner, and homebody has made the sandwich part of his or her American lunch lifestyle. And because the sandwich is such an appealing lunch-time dish, it can be served with equal success at a businessmen's buffet lunch, ladies' luncheon, Saturday-noon family get-together, or to anyone (even just yourself) any day when the clock strikes twelve.

There are all kinds of tempting sandwiches in this chapter. Some can be made ahead, some take only a few minutes to put together, and others take a little more time for the person who enjoys and has time to do a little more meal preparation. Both open-faced and closed sandwiches are included, as well as hot and cold ones. Look for famous sandwiches, such as Croque Monsieur, as well as innovative ones, such as the Gazpacho Sandwich or Beety Beef Fries ("topless" sautéed hamburger-type sandwiches that blush slightly at the idea themselves).

Chances are you won't want to serve meat at lunch every day, so a good number of the sandwiches in this chapter make ample use of cheese, vegetables, eggs, and fish. Many of the recipes in Chapter 8 can also be used in your lunch menu, especially if you serve them with a soup or salad. Suggestions are at the end of recipes for accompanying foods that will make your menu truly enticing.

THE REUBEN SANDWICH

The Reuben may well be the best-known American sandwich, at least in the Northeast. Whether it was originally made with sauerkraut or cole slaw, with or without a slice of turkey added to the corned beef, or served open-faced or closed, is a matter for debate. But that Reuben's Restaurant in New York came up with a real sandwich winner is a matter of fact. The recipe below is my version of the ideal Reuben.

4 large slices rye bread
softened butter or margarine
Russian dressing (bought, or see Index)
¾ pound corned beef, thinly sliced
½ pound thoroughly drained sauerkraut
4 large slices Swiss or Gruyère cheese

Preheat oven at 400°. Toast bread lightly and butter it. Cover the buttered side with Russian dressing. Arrange corned beef over dressing. Arrange sauerkraut over corned beef. Arrange cheese over sauerkraut. Arrange sandwiches on a baking sheet. Heat in oven 5–7 minutes until heated through and cheese begins to melt. Run under broiler a minute or so to brown the cheese. Cut in half and serve immediately.

Makes 4 servings.

MENU SUGGESTION: While the Reuben is really a meal in itself, you might want to serve it with such pickles as Peter Piper's Fresh Pickled Sweet Green Peppers (see Index) and steins of beer or ale.

SYRIAN SPECIAL

1 28-ounce can Italian tomatoes
⅓ cup pine nuts (pignolias)
2 tablespoons vegetable oil
1½ cups chopped onion
1 pound ground lamb
¼ cup chopped parsley
¼ cup very finely chopped green pepper
2 tablespoons lemon juice
1 tablespoon vinegar
1 teaspoon salt
¼ teaspoon ground allspice
cayenne pepper to taste
4 whole wheat (or white) pita breads (see In-
    dex or use bought pita)

Drain the tomatoes and chop them, reserving liquid for another use. You will have about 1½ cups
chopped tomatoes. Set aside.

In a heavy skillet lightly brown the pine nuts in 1
tablespoon oil, stirring constantly. Remove pine nuts
with a slotted spoon and put in a small bowl.

Add tomatoes to the skillet and cook, stirring,
about 5 minutes, until thickened. Add to the pine nuts.
Return skillet to stove and add remaining oil. Sauté
onions until soft. Add lamb and cook, breaking up meat
and stirring until it loses its red color. Add parsley,
green pepper, lemon juice, vinegar, salt, allspice, and
cayenne pepper, and cook, stirring, about 3 minutes.
Add the tomato–pine nut mixture and continue to cook,
stirring, another minute or two. Remove from heat. Slit
pita breads open at edge about ⅓ of the way around.

Stuff with meat mixture, dividing equally. Serve immediately.

Makes 4.

MENU SUGGESTION: Serve with peppermint tea and have
yogurt (any flavor you like) to top it off.

GERMAN LIVERWURST CAPRICE

½ medium-size cucumber, cut in half length-
    wise, seeded and shredded (peeled if cu-
    cumber was waxed)
4 radishes, thinly sliced
2 tablespoons vinegar
salt
freshly ground pepper
softened butter or margarine
4 slices German pumpernickel or other
    pumpernickel
½ pound (or more) liverwurst
Boston lettuce or similar buttery-type lettuce
2 3-ounce packages cream cheese, softened
4 slices crispbread
paprika

Combine cucumber, radish slices, and vinegar.
Sprinkle with salt and pepper, cover, and refrigerate 1
hour or longer. Drain well.

Butter pumpernickel and spread thickly with liverwurst. Cover with a layer of lettuce. Spread cream
cheese on crispbread. Set crispbread on top of liverwurst. Top each sandwich with ¼ drained cucumber
mixture. Sprinkle lightly with paprika. Serve immediately.

Makes 4.

MENU SUGGESTION: Serve with a pot of mustard for those
who might like to spread some on the liverwurst. German or
domestic beer or buttermilk to drink.

CHAPPATI WITH EGGPLANT TAHINI

8 or more chappati (see Index)
1 large or 2 small eggplants
1 cup cooked or canned drained chickpeas
    (garbanzos)
1/2 cup tahini (ground sesame seed)
1/4 cup lemon juice
2 garlic cloves, minced
1/4 cup vegetable oil
1 1/2 teaspoons salt
pepper to taste
2 scallions, including some of green part,
    finely sliced
1 tablespoon chopped parsley

Prepare chappati to use as sandwich bases. Preheat oven at 400°. Prick eggplant all over with tines of a fork. Set on a baking sheet and bake about 35 minutes until soft, turning a few times. Remove from oven and place eggplant in a bowl of cold water. Cut off stem end and peel off skin from stem end down. Cut up eggplant and drain well in colander. Place in food processor or blender along with chickpeas, tahini, lemon juice, garlic, oil, salt, and pepper, and blend until smooth. Spread on chappati and sprinkle scallions and parsley over each. Serve immediately. (Eggplant mixture can also be chilled and the sandwiches served cold.)

Makes 8 or more, depending on how thickly you spread filling.

MENU SUGGESTION: Spinach-and-sliced-mushroom salad.

CROQUE MONSIEUR

France's most famous sandwich, and probably the most popular one there, Croque Monsieur is easy to prepare and makes not only a luscious lunch but an equally nice snack, especially a late-night bite. Cut into little squares, it's an excellent cocktail sandwich.

2 thin slices firm white bread (such as Pep- peridge Farm Very Thin Sliced White Bread)
1 thin slice Gruyère cheese (not processed Gruyère)
1 thin slice ham
clarified butter (see Index)

Cover 1 slice bread with a slice of Gruyère. Cover Gruyère with a slice of ham. Cover ham with another slice of Gruyère. Cover with another slice of bread. Trim crusts (save all the trimmings for nibbling). With palm of your hand or with a small flat board, press down firmly. Brush top of sandwich with clarified butter. Coat a large, heavy frying pan or skillet heavily with clarified butter and put sandwich, buttered side down, in skillet over low heat. Brush top with clarified butter. Sauté until crisp and nicely browned on both sides, turning. Serve immediately.

Makes 1 sandwich. You can make as many sandwiches at a time as will fit into your frying pan or skillet.

MENU SUGGESTION: Salad of halved cherry tomatoes marinated in oil-and-vinegar dressing, or other preferred dressing, to which a little basil has been added.

CROQUE MADAME

While some people think of Croque Madame as a postscript to Croque Monsieur, the sandwiches really have no relationship to each other. Croque Madame stands alone, an open-faced chicken creation covered with a rich blending of three cheeses, two of them in the sauce that bubbles and browns the top.

1 egg
1 tablespoon quick-mixing or instant flour
   (such as Gold Medal Wondra)
¼ cup white wine
freshly ground pepper to taste
½ cup grated Parmesan cheese
½ cup grated Cheddar cheese
1 loaf Italian bread
softened butter or margarine
⅓–½ pound cold sliced cooked chicken
thin slices Beaumont or Port Salut cheese

Beat egg lightly with wire whisk. Beat in flour with wire whisk. Mix in wine and pepper. Add Parmesan and Cheddar cheeses and mix well. Cover and refrigerate 1 hour.

Preheat oven at 450°. Cut 1 lengthwise slice, ¾ inch thick, from bottom of Italian bread. (Reserve remaining bread for another use.) Toast the cut side and butter it. Arrange sliced chicken on top. Arrange a few slices of Beaumont or Port Salut cheese over chicken. Set sandwich on baking sheet. Spoon refrigerated sauce over entire sandwich. Bake about 15 minutes until nicely browned. Cut crosswise into 3 or 4 pieces and serve immediately.

Makes 3 or 4 servings. To make 6 or 8 servings cut 2 slices from the bread and toast all cut sides. Double other ingredients in recipe and proceed as above.

MENU SUGGESTION: Romaine salad.

GAZPACHO SANDWICH

Gazpacho converted into a sandwich is as lovely and cooling as its namesake soup.

**4 white mountain rolls, or other large rolls
with firm but not hard crust
softened butter or margarine
2 medium-size or 3 small tomatoes, peeled and
thinly sliced
1 cucumber, thinly sliced
1 tablespoon finely chopped onion
2 tablespoons finely chopped green pepper
vinaigrette dressing (see Index), or any oil-
and-vinegar dressing**

Slice rolls in half horizontally. Hollow out tops and bottoms, leaving a thin shell. (Reserve soft crumbs for another use.) Butter inside of rolls. Put tops and bottoms together, wrap in plastic wrap, and refrigerate.

Combine tomato slices, cucumber slices, onion, and green pepper in a bowl. Pour enough vinaigrette dressing over the vegetables to moisten well, and toss. Cover and refrigerate 1 hour or longer, turning once or twice. Drain.

Fill rolls with gazpacho filling, dividing equally. Replace tops. Cut in half if desired. Serve immediately. Makes 4 servings.

MENU SUGGESTION: Chickpeas and salami strips marinated in a creamy dressing.

HAMMY HERB-MUSTARD HAMBURGERS

½ stick butter or margarine
4 teaspoons Dijon mustard
1 tablespoon chopped parsley
1 cup chopped onion
1 tablespoon vegetable oil
1 pound ground beef
1 cup finely chopped cooked ham
¼ teaspoon thyme
kosher salt or other coarse salt
4 seeded hard rolls

Soften butter and beat until creamy. Add mustard and parsley and mix well. Set aside.

Sauté onions in oil until soft. Remove from pan and combine with ground beef, ham, and thyme. Form into 4 patties.

Heat skillet over high flame and sprinkle a teaspoon or so of salt evenly over surface of pan. Brown hamburgers quickly on one side. Turn, reduce heat to low, and cook to desired degree of doneness.

Meanwhile, slice rolls in half and toast cut sides. Spread toasted sides with the butter-mustard mixture. When hamburgers are ready, put between roll halves. Serve immediately.

Makes 4.

MENU SUGGESTION: Florinda's Olive Salad (see Index).

GOLDEN TONGUE SANDWICH

3 hard-cooked eggs
¼ pound thinly sliced cooked tongue
2 tablespoons chopped pimiento-stuffed olives
2 tablespoons pickle relish or chopped sweet
   pickle
⅓ cup mayonnaise
1 tablespoon lemon juice
½ stick softened butter or margarine
4 teaspoons Dijon mustard
8 slices Black Peasant Bread (see Index) or
   similar dark bread

Chop the hard-cooked eggs and tongue. Combine with chopped olives and pickle relish. Combine mayonnaise and lemon juice and add to the tongue mixture. Cream butter and add the mustard. Butter the bread slices with the mixture. Make sandwiches with the egg-tongue filling, and cut in half.

Makes 4.

MENU SUGGESTION: Caponata, also called eggplant appetizer. (See Index or purchase in cans—Progresso is a good brand.)

PAPAGO CHILI POPOVERS

Whether you make your chili searingly hot or very mild, be sure to serve lots of ice-cold beer with Papago Chili Popovers. The hotter the chili, the more beer you'll be likely to drink.

For the chili:
> 4 cans chili con carne without beans, plus
>   chili powder to taste, or:
> 2 medium onions, chopped
> 1 tablespoon vegetable oil
> 1½ pounds ground beef
> 1 17-ounce can Italian tomatoes
> 2 tablespoons chopped parsley
> 1 garlic clove, chopped
> 2 or more tablespoons chili powder
> 1 teaspoon cumin seed, ground
> 1 teaspoon salt
> dash cayenne pepper
> 1 teaspoon vinegar
> 2 tablespoons masa harina* or flour

For the popovers:
> 1 cup milk
> ½ teaspoon salt
> about 2½ cups flour
> 5 teaspoons baking powder
> fat for deep frying
> 1 cup sour cream

---

* Masa harina is a fine-textured cornmeal product which is ideal for thickening chili. It is available in stores that sell Mexican- or Spanish-type products.

If using canned chili, empty into saucepan, add chili powder, and simmer until hot and somewhat thickened. If the chili is too thin, boil it down or add a little flour mixed with water and heat a little longer.

If making your own chili (which you can do a day or two ahead if you like), fry onions in oil until lightly browned. Remove from pan. Cook meat in same pan, breaking up with a fork, until it looses its red color. Return onions to the pan with the meat and add tomatoes, parsley, garlic, chili powder, cumin, salt, cayenne pepper, and vinegar, and mix well. Simmer, covered, 1½ hours, stirring occasionally and breaking up the tomatoes. Mix masa harina or flour with a little water and add to chili, stirring constantly. Continue stirring until thickened, and simmer another 15 minutes, stirring occasionally. Cover and store in refrigerator until ready to reheat for serving.

Combine milk and salt and add enough flour to make a smooth bread dough. Work the dough, pulling with the fingers, until stretchy. Blend in baking powder with a spoon or with fingers. With floured hands form dough into egg-size balls and set on a tray lined with wax paper or plastic wrap.

Heat fat in a wok or deep fryer until hot but not smoking. Take one ball of dough at a time and stretch with the hands into as large a circle as you can make. It should be at least the size of a lunch plate, and ideally the size of a dinner plate. Fry until brown on one side; turn and brown other side. Drain on paper towels. Continue until all dough balls have been stretched, fried, and drained. Spoon hot chili over each popover and top with a dollop of sour cream. Serve immediately. Eat with the fingers.

Makes about 1 dozen popovers and filling for 8–10. Eat the extra popovers "as is" or drizzle them with honey.

DELI TRIPLE TREAT

8 ounces cream cheese
1/4 cup sour cream
2 tablespoons snipped fresh chives
1/2 teaspoon salt
5 hard-cooked eggs
10 sliced pitted black olives
1/2 teaspoon salt
pepper to taste
mayonnaise
24 thin slices Jewish rye bread
softened butter or margarine
6 or more slices (depending on size of fish)
   lox or Nova Scotia salmon

Soften cream cheese in a bowl. Add sour cream and mix well. Add chives and salt, mix well, cover, and refrigerate 4 hours or longer.

Meanwhile, chop the hard-cooked eggs. Add olives, salt and pepper, and enough mayonnaise to moisten. Cover and refrigerate.

Lay out 6 slices of bread. Spread with cream cheese—chive mixture. Lay out 6 more slices of bread and butter them. Arrange, butter side up, over cream cheese. Arrange a layer of lox or salmon on sandwiches, trimming to fit the bread. Lay out 6 more slices of bread and butter them. Arrange over lox, buttered side down. Spread egg mixture on top. Cover with remaining bread slices. Cut each sandwich into quarters with a very sharp knife. Makes 6.

MENU SUGGESTION: Kosher dill pickles, pickled green tomatoes, or Mother's Green Tomato Pickles (see Index).

UKRAINIAN HRINKY

This is a French-toasted chopped liver sandwich, which makes a very hearty lunch when accompanied by a steaming bowl of mushroom-and-barley soup.

2 tablespoons grated onion
1 tablespoon butter or margarine
1 cup ground cooked calves' liver (about ½ pound)
½ teaspoon salt
pepper to taste
½ cup béchamel sauce (see Index)
4 or 6 slices firm white bread
1 egg
¼ cup milk
fine dry breadcrumbs
clarified butter (see Index)

Sauté grated onion in butter until lightly browned. Remove from stove. Add liver, salt, pepper, and béchamel. Spread on 2 or 3 bread slices and cover with remaining slices, pressing down lightly. Cut each sandwich into 3 or 4 triangles, depending on size of bread.

Beat egg lightly in a shallow soup plate and add milk. Place breadcrumbs in another shallow soup plate. Dip each sandwich triangle in egg mixture, then in breadcrumbs, coating all sides. Brown on all sides in clarified butter. Serve immediately.

Makes 2 or 3 sandwiches (8–12 triangles).

ORIENTAL WONDER

¼ cup tahini (ground sesame seed)
1 tablespoon miso (soy bean paste) or soy
    sauce (preferably tamari soy sauce)
1 tablespoon lemon juice
4 slices Westphalian pumpernickel
1 small apple, cored and cut in thin slices
1 cup bean sprouts
2 to 4 leaves Boston lettuce or other buttery-
    type lettuce

Mix together tahini, miso or soy sauce, and lemon juice. Mixture thickens when combined. Spread on bread slices. Arrange apple slices on 2 pieces of the bread and pile bean sprouts on top. Cover with lettuce and remaining bread slices. Cut in half.

Makes 2.

MENU SUGGESTION: Serve with glasses of cranberry juice and follow up with ripe bananas for a delicious meatless lunch.

FRAN'S PRIZE-WINNING CHOPPED CHICKEN LIVER ON BIALY

1 pound chicken livers
2 large onions, chopped
4 tablespoons rendered chicken fat
1 envelope MBT Instant Beef Broth or 1
    beef bouillon cube
3 hard-cooked eggs
salt
pepper
6–8 bialys or onion rolls
Boston lettuce or other buttery-type lettuce
    (optional)

Drop chicken livers into a pot of boiling water and boil until pinky-brown. Remove with slotted spoon and set aside.

Sauté onions in 3 tablespoons chicken fat, adding the MBT or bouillon cube, until onions are golden.

Chop onions, eggs, and chicken livers together (preferably in wooden bowl with chopper, but in any case do not grind them). Add a little salt and pepper to taste. Mix in the remaining chicken fat. Chill.

Slit bialys in half and make sandwiches with the chicken liver filling. Top with lettuce leaves if desired. Close and cut in half.

Makes 6–8 or more, depending on size of rolls and how thickly you spread on filling.

MENU SUGGESTION: Deli Salad (see Index) or mixed-vegetable salad from delicatessen.

KEFTEDES SANDWICH

Keftedes are Greek meatballs which make a very delicious sandwich filling. Round out a Greek-style menu with macaroni salad and a white retsina wine.

1 egg
1 cup firm white breadcrumbs
½ pound ground beef
½ pound ground lamb, veal, or pork
1 large onion, grated
1 tablespoon tomato paste
¼ cup white wine
1 garlic clove, finely minced
½ teaspoon oregano
1 teaspoon chopped fresh mint or dried
    mint
flour
1 tablespoon or more olive oil
1 tablespoon or more butter or margarine
10 French rolls (oblong hard rolls)

Beat the egg lightly. Add breadcrumbs and mix well. Add beef and lamb, veal, or pork, and mix well. Add onion, tomato paste, wine, garlic, oregano, and mint, and work together until well combined. Cover and refrigerate 1 hour or longer.

Form into 1-inch balls. Flatten slightly. Dredge with flour. Fry in oil and butter until nicely browned all over, adding more oil and butter if necessary. Meanwhile, cut rolls open lengthwise without cutting all the way through. Pull out some of soft center and reserve for another use. When meatballs are ready, put 4 in each roll, along with some of the pan drippings. Serve immediately. Makes 10 servings.

CHICKEN DIVAN SANDWICH

Oatmeal Bread (see Index) or any preferred
    bread
butter or margarine
cold sliced cooked chicken breast (allow 1
    pound for 6 sandwiches)
salt
Italian Fontina cheese (if not available use
    Beaumont or Port Salut)
broccoli spears cooked until just crisp
        tender (split each lengthwise into 2 or 3
        pieces, depending on size of spear)
    slivered almonds
    mornay sauce (see Index)

Preheat oven at 350°. Toast 1 slice of bread for
each serving you wish to make. Butter the toast. Arrange chicken on each piece. Sprinkle lightly with salt.
Arrange a thin slice of cheese over chicken. Arrange 2
strips of broccoli on each sandwich, cutting to fit. Arrange sandwiches on aluminum-foil-lined baking sheet.
Sprinkle almonds on sandwiches and spoon mornay
sauce over almonds. Bake 10–15 minutes. Run under
broiler a minute or two to brown tops. Serve immediately.

MENU SUGGESTION: Serve with white wine.

PISTO DE ARAGÓN SANDWICH

2 garlic cloves, finely chopped
¼ cup vegetable oil
2 medium-size zucchini, sliced very thin
2 medium-size potatoes, peeled, halved,
    and sliced very thin
2 medium-size onions, sliced very thin
1 green pepper, cut in quarters and sliced
    crosswise very thin
1 teaspoon salt
3 fresh or canned stewed tomatoes, drained
3 eggs
6 hard rolls

In a large frying pan heat garlic and oil together until oil begins to bubble around garlic. Add zucchini, potatoes, onions, green pepper, and salt, and sauté, turning vegetables over frequently, until tender and lightly browned, 15 minutes or more.

Mash the tomatoes and add them to the frying pan, mixing well. Beat the eggs and add to the frying pan, stirring with a wooden spoon until mixture is well blended and eggs are set. Remove from stove.

Cut rolls in half and pull out soft inner part and reserve for another use. Fill rolls with the vegetable mixture. Serve immediately, or cover vegetable mixture, refrigerate until serving time, and fill the rolls with the cold mixture. Unbeatable either way.

Makes 6.

MENU SUGGESTION: Nice with a glass of red wine.

TOFU-SHRIMP STUFFED PITA

3 tablespoons soy sauce (preferably tamari
    soy sauce)
1 tablespoon vegetable oil (preferably
    sesame oil)
2 tablespoons lemon juice
1½ cups chilled cooked shrimp (about 6
    ounces), cut up
4 tablespoons chopped scallions, including
    some of green part
¼ pound tofu (bean curd—available
    fresh or canned at health-food, specialty
    stores, and Oriental food shops)
2 cups shredded lettuce
4 pita breads (preferably whole wheat—
    see Index or use bought pita)

Combine soy sauce, oil, and lemon juice. Add
shrimp and scallions. Cut bean curd into cubes about
¼ inch square. Add bean curd and lettuce to shrimp
mixture and toss gently. Slit pita breads open about
⅓ of the way around edges. Stuff with shrimp-tofu
mixture.

Makes 4.

MENU SUGGESTION: Serve small bowls of egg drop soup
before you serve the stuffed pita.

BEETY BEEF FRIES

6–8 slices granola bread or similar bread
butter or margarine
2 egg yolks
¾ pound lean ground beef
2 tablespoons grated onion
1¼–1½ cups finely chopped boiled potato
    (1 medium potato)
¾ cup finely chopped pickled beets,
    drained
1 tablespoon capers
½ teaspoon salt

Butter bread on one side and sauté until golden. Set aside.

Beat egg yolks until thick and pale. Add ground beef and mix well. Add onion, potato, beets, capers, and salt, and mix until well blended. Spread evenly over unfried sides of bread.

Melt a tablespoon or two of butter in the skillet and sauté the sandwiches, meat side down, until nicely browned. Serve immediately, meat side up.

Makes 6–8, depending on size of bread used.

MENU SUGGESTION: Asparagus vinaigrette (see Index for vinaigrette dressing or use any vinegar-and-oil dressing).

NEW ORLEANS MUFFULETTA

This is a favorite lunch-time sandwich in New Orleans, where authentic Muffulettas are made and sold daily at the Progress Grocery Company as well as the Central Grocery Company, both on Decatur Street in the heart of the French Quarter. The Progress Grocery Company is a lovely old wooden-shelved grocery store where beans and other staples are sold out of open burlap sacks and the fragrance of cheeses and other delectable foods fills the air. They've been making the Muffuletta (pronounced moo-fa-letta) in the French Quarter for over 60 years and at the Progress Grocery Company for over 50 years. The outstanding feature of the sandwich is the delicious olive salad it contains, and Muffulettas are equally good whether you eat them indoors for lunch or outdoors at picnics or football games as many people in New Orleans do. Mr. John Perrone, proprietor of the Progress Grocery Company, has kindly shared the recipe for this outstanding sandwich.

1 cup drained finely chopped mixed pickled
    vegetables (giardiniera in vinegar—
    available where Italian foods are sold)
1⅓ cups finely chopped celery
⅔ cup finely chopped pitted Sicilian green
    olives
¼ cup olive oil
1 garlic clove, finely minced (optional)
2 tablespoons chopped parsley (optional)
½ teaspoon oregano (optional)
freshly ground pepper to taste (optional)

**3 round loaves Italian bread, 8 inches in
diameter**
**¾ pound sliced lean ham (preferably
Polish ham)**
¾ pound sliced provolone cheese
¾ pound sliced Genoa salami

Combine pickled vegetables, celery, and olives in a glass or ceramic bowl. Add oil and toss well. If desired add any or all of optional ingredients, that is, garlic, oregano, pepper, and parsley, and toss again. Cover and refrigerate 8 hours or overnight, tossing once or twice during that time.

Cut loaves of bread in half horizontally. (If any loaf is more than 2 inches high remove a slice from the center and reserve for another use so that height is reduced to between 1½ and 2 inches.) Brush cut sides of bread with some of the oil from the olive mixture. Arrange ham on 3 bottom sections of bread, dividing equally. Cover with provolone cheese, dividing equally. Cover with Genoa salami, dividing equally. Spoon olive mixture over salami, dividing equally. Close sandwiches and cut each in half. Serve a half to each person.

Makes 6 servings.

MENU SUGGESTION: The Muffuletta is very substantial and almost a meal in itself. All you need is some beer, wine, coffee, soft drink, or whatever you like to drink with it.

5. SANDWICHES FOR BRUNCH TIME

To make the morning precious.
—JOHN KEATS, *"Sleep and Poetry"*

Brunch is becoming an increasingly popular meal, and perhaps the most enjoyable of any, because it's served at a relaxed time, usually on Sunday, when blessed leisure hours stretch before you.

No food is so tailor-made for brunch time as the sandwich, and the recipes in this chapter run the gamut from the favorite classic French-fried Monte Cristo Sandwich, stuffed with ham, cheese, and chicken, to new and lively sandwiches like Tipsy Sardines with Mushrooms on Toast. You'll find unusual sandwiches made with English muffins, corn sticks, tortillas, and toast cups. Fillings range from the simple (eggs) to the sublime (frogs' legs), with stops in between to suit every taste. You may find other recipes in other chapters of this book to be equally attractive for brunch —by all means, try them. Stuffed Brioche Wedges, for example, is a lovely brunch idea.

Serve your brunch-time sandwiches with piping-hot coffee, good tea, or steaming chocolate. Start off with juices or, for a more spirited repast, Bloody Marys, Screwdrivers, Salty Dogs (grapefruit juice with vodka and a dash of salt), or any other cocktail that seems appealing for the first meal of the day. If you want to go all out, serve champagne or a chilled white wine with your brunch. Suggestions for rounding out your menu follow the recipes.

ORANGE AND CANADIAN BACON
ENGLISH MUFFINS

12 slices Canadian bacon
6 thin slices onion
2 large or 3 medium oranges
1 tablespoon cornstarch
1 cup orange juice
1 teaspoon grated lemon peel
6 English muffins or 12 crumpets (see
    Index)
softened butter or margarine

Preheat oven at 300°. Arrange 6 slices Canadian bacon on a greased baking sheet. Place an onion slice on each. Cut rind off oranges so that all membrane is removed. Cut 6 orange slices about ½ inch thick from the centers of the oranges. Remove any seeds. Lay an orange slice on each onion slice. Top with remaining Canadian bacon slices. Bake 25 minutes.

Meanwhile, put cornstarch in a saucepan. Add orange juice gradually and stir until smooth. Cut up the remaining orange pieces into small pieces. Cook the juice, stirring, until thickened. Add the orange pieces and lemon peel and cook for about a minute more over low heat. Turn off heat.

Split, toast, and butter English muffins, or toast and butter crumpets. Arrange on serving plates. Arrange bacon groups on muffins. Spoon orange sauce over each, dividing sauce equally. Close and eat with hands, or leave open-faced and eat with knife and fork.

Makes 6.

MENU SUGGESTION: Prune-whip yogurt.

CHILI SCRAMBLED EGGS IN CORN-STICK SANDWICHES

corn sticks (see Index)
4 eggs
1 teaspoon chili powder
2 tablespoons milk
softened butter or margarine

Bake corn sticks and turn out on wire rack to cool slightly while preparing eggs. Beat eggs with milk and chili powder. Melt about a tablespoon of butter in a skillet and scramble the eggs. Cut corn sticks in half horizontally. Butter bottom halves lightly. Spoon eggs onto corn sticks. Close and serve immediately.

Makes enough filling for 6 large corn sticks, or 3 servings of 2 corn sticks each.

MENU SUGGESTION: Vegetable-juice cocktail, sausage or grilled ham.

IRISH SEEDY BREAD BACON SANDWICH

When the Irish put seeds in their renowned soda bread they call it seedy bread. It makes a wonderful brunch bread when toasted and buttered, and is even better sandwiching slices of crisp bacon. In Ireland on St. Patrick's Day, the dish of the day is not corned beef but bacon, with cabbage. So what could be more inventively Irish than seedy bread with bacon?

Irish Seedy Bread (see Index)
softened butter or margarine
sliced bacon (allow 4 or more slices per
    sandwich)

Slice bread fairly thick. Grill or fry bacon and while draining on paper towels, toast and butter bread. Make sandwiches with the bacon, cut in half, and serve immediately.

A loaf of Irish Seedy Bread will make 7 or more sandwiches.

MENU SUGGESTION: Irish oatmeal and Irish Breakfast tea. For a very special brunch, start with Irish coffee.

MONTE CRISTO SANDWICH

**9 slices firm white bread ¼ inch thick
(such as Pepperidge Farm Very Thin
Sliced White Bread)
butter or margarine, softened
3 slices lean ham (if sliced very thin, use 6
slices)
3 slices cooked chicken, preferably white
meat
3 slices Swiss or Gruyère cheese (not
processed Gruyère)
1 egg
2 tablespoons milk
⅛ teaspoon salt
freshly ground pepper**

For each sandwich make a stack of 3 bread slices and trim off crusts evenly. Butter 2 of the slices for each sandwich. Between each of the 2 buttered slices place a layer of ham covered by a layer of chicken, making sure the meat does not extend beyond the bread. Place cheese on top, making sure it does not extend beyond the bread, and cover with the remaining bread slice. Beat the egg lightly in a flat soup plate and stir in the milk, salt, and pepper.

Melt 2 tablespoons butter in a skillet over a low-to-medium flame. Holding together with the fingers, dip sandwiches, one at a time, top and bottom, in the egg mixture. Do not dip sides. Sauté on one side until nicely browned. Turn carefully, turn heat to very low, and cover skillet. Allow to cook until cheese has melted and sandwiches are brown on bottom. Transfer to serving plates and cut sandwiches in halves or quarters.

Serve immediately.
Makes 3.

MENU SUGGESTION: Serve with whole-berry cranberry sauce, Cranberry Chutney (see Index), or Orange Pickled Walnut Chutney (see Index).

CURRIED MUSHROOMS ON POPPADOMS

1 pound mushrooms
3 tablespoons clarified butter (see Index)
1 cup thinly sliced onion
1/4 teaspoon finely chopped fresh ginger
    root or canned green ginger root
1/2 teaspoon turmeric
1/2 teaspoon salt
pinch each of chili powder, freshly ground
    black pepper, ground coriander, caraway
    seeds, ground cloves, ground cardamom,
    cinnamon
1 teaspoon lemon juice
4 plain poppadoms*
vegetable oil
4 teaspoons chopped parsley

* Poppadoms, which look something like very thin tortillas, come from India and can be bought in packages of 5 ounces or more (a 5-ounce package contains about 20 poppadoms). They come in several flavors, but the plain ones are best for this sandwich. Poppadoms can be purchased at specialty food stores, Indian-food stores and gift shops, and some supermarkets and grocery stores. You may note that the spelling of poppadoms is not always the same and varies from one brand to another.

Clean and cut mushrooms in quarters or halves, leaving tiny mushrooms whole, so that all pieces are of uniform size. Heat butter in skillet and sauté onion and ginger root about 5 minutes, turning, until onion is soft. Add turmeric, salt, and chili powder, and cook a minute longer, stirring.

Add mushrooms and cook, stirring and tossing continually, for 15 minutes. After the first five minutes or so the mushrooms will begin to exude moisture and you will not need to be quite so diligent in the stirring and tossing, since there will be no further danger of scorching. Add the remaining spices and lemon juice and simmer another minute or two, stirring. Turn off flame.

To prepare poppadoms follow directions on package or proceed as follows: In another skillet heat ¼ inch to ½ inch oil until hot but not smoking. Do not allow oil to become too hot. Fry the poppadoms one at a time for a few seconds on each side. They will puff up immediately. The entire operation should not take more than 5 or 6 seconds for each poppadom. Drain on paper towels.

Spoon the mushroom mixture equally over the poppadoms and sprinkle with chopped parsley. Serve immediately. These can be eaten with a fork but are much more fun to pick up and eat by hand. Either way they're sensational.

Makes 4.

MENU SUGGESTION: Precede with broiled honeyed grapefruit.

SAUSAGE SANDWICH WITH SAUTÉED APPLE SLICES

3 large pork sausages
1 large or 2 small hard apples
butter or margarine
2 slices whole wheat bread or other
    whole-grain bread
maple syrup

Split sausages in half lengthwise. Brown slowly in skillet, turning often and draining fat off as it collects, until brown and cooked through, about 15 minutes.

Meanwhile, cut the apples into thick slices and, in another skillet, sauté in butter over low heat, turning often, until nicely browned and tender. They should be brown at the same time the sausages are ready.

Toast bread and butter it. Drain sausages and arrange on toast. Arrange apple slices over sausages. Pour maple syrup over all. Serve immediately. Eat with knife and fork. (If you wish to make sandwiches that you can pick up, make closed sandwiches using 4 slices of toast, and cut in half.)

Makes 2.

MENU SUGGESTION: For a really hearty meal, serve scrambled eggs on the side.

SWISS BAKED EGGS IN TOAST CUPS

6 slices soft white bread
butter or margarine
4 slices bacon
6 eggs
⅓ cup (approximately) grated or shredded
   Swiss cheese
paprika
salt and pepper to taste

Preheat oven at 400°. Remove crusts from bread slices without removing any of the bread itself, if possible. Lightly butter 6 depressions of a muffin tin. Mold one slice of bread into each of the depressions, shaping with the fingers to form bread cups. If necessary, fill in any missing sections toward the top of the cups with other pieces of soft white bread. Set in oven for 3–5 minutes, until lightly browned. Remove from oven but leave toast cups in the muffin tin.

Fry bacon just long enough to brown slightly and remove some of the fat. The bacon should still be limp. Drain on paper towel and cut each strip crosswise into 3 pieces. Crisscross 2 pieces of bacon in the bottom of each toast cup. Separate the eggs, putting each yolk in a separate cup and the whites together in a bowl. Working quickly, transfer a yolk in each toast cup over the bacon and spoon some of the white into the remaining space in each cup. Put in oven for 2 minutes. Sprinkle some cheese over each egg and bake another 10 minutes. Remove from oven and sprinkle with paprika. Serve 1 or 2 to each person. Let each person sprinkle with salt and pepper to taste. Makes 6 (3–6 servings).

MENU SUGGESTION: Peach nectar.

CRABS ON CRUMPETS

1½ tablespoons butter or margarine
1½ tablespoons flour
¾ cup milk
¼ teaspoon salt
freshly ground pepper to taste
1 tablespoon brandy
1 tablespoon chopped parsley
1 tablespoon toasted slivered almonds
1 egg, lightly beaten
1 cup lump crabmeat or canned crabmeat,
     picked over
4 crumpets (bought or see Index) or 2 split
     English muffins
softened butter or margarine

Melt butter in a saucepan and stir in the flour with a wire whisk. Add milk all at once and stir with wire whisk. Heat until thickened and bubbly, stirring constantly. Remove from heat. Add salt, pepper, brandy, parsley, and almonds, and mix well. Add egg and crabmeat and mix again. Return to stove over low heat. Allow to heat while toasting and buttering crumpets or English muffins. Arrange 1 crumpet on each serving plate and spoon hot crab mixture over top. Serve immediately.

This may also be made as a closed sandwich, using 8 crumpets or 4 English muffins.

Makes 4.

MENU SUGGESTION: Fresh figs in season, or canned whole figs.

FRENCH-TOASTED CHALLAH SANDWICH WITH TART CHERRIES AND CREAM CHEESE

1 3-ounce package cream cheese
1½ tablespoons milk or cream
1 tablespoon sugar
¾ cup canned tart red pitted cherries,
    drained
1 loaf challah (bought or see Index)
2 eggs
¼ cup milk
¼ teaspoon salt
butter or margarine

Cream the cream cheese and add milk or cream a little at a time until thoroughly blended. Add the sugar and mix well. Add the cherries and toss well. Set aside.

Cut 3 slices challah 1½ inches thick and cut in half lengthwise. Trim crusts if desired. Beat eggs lightly in a shallow soup plate. Add milk and salt.

Melt 2 tablespoons butter in a skillet. Dip the bread pieces in egg mixture on all sides and sauté, 3 at a time, in the butter, adding more butter as necessary, to make French toast. Slit the French toast horizontally with a sharp knife, without cutting all the way through, to form a pocket. Spoon cream cheese–cherry mixture into pockets, dividing equally among the 6 pieces. You will need to do a little forcing to get the filling all in. Serve immediately.

Makes 6 servings.

MENU SUGGESTION: Pineapple juice.

HERRING BAGELWICH

1 8-ounce jar herring party snacks in wine
   sauce
4 onion bagels
butter or margarine
1 3-ounce package cream cheese
3 tablespoons chopped dill pickle or other
   sour pickle
Boston lettuce or other buttery-type
   lettuce, shredded (optional)

Drain herring well. Cut herring and onions which come in the jar into fine slivers. Split, toast, and butter the bagels. Spread lightly with cream cheese. Divide the herring-and-onion evenly and arrange over the cream cheese. Divide the chopped pickle evenly and arrange over the herring. Cover with shredded lettuce if desired. Cut tops of bagels in half and place on top of sandwiches. Then cut all the way through the sandwiches. This way of cutting the sandwiches prevents the filling from oozing out.

Makes 4.

MENU SUGGESTION: Applesauce sprinkled with cinnamon, or apple juice.

BRANDIED LOBSTER SANDWICH

1 tablespoon butter or margarine
1½ tablespoons flour
¾ cup milk
1 tablespoon tomato paste
2 tablespoons brandy
1 tablespoon chopped parsley
½ teaspoon salt
pinch of nutmeg
pinch of tarragon
pepper to taste
1 cup cooked lobster cut into small pieces
    (about ¼ pound)
4 slices firm white bread
softened butter or margarine
¼ cup or more shredded Gruyère cheese
    (not processed Gruyère) or similar
    cheese such as Swiss or Jarlsberg

Melt butter in saucepan and stir in flour with a wire whisk. Add milk all at once and stir with wire whisk. Heat until thickened and bubbly, stirring constantly. Remove from heat. Add tomato paste and mix well. Add brandy, parsley, salt, nutmeg, tarragon, and pepper, and mix again. Add lobster meat, return to stove and simmer gently about 3 minutes, stirring occasionally.

Preheat broiler. Arrange bread slices on baking sheet and toast on one side under broiler. Turn and butter the untoasted side. Spoon the lobster mixture over toast. Sprinkle each with 1 or more tablespoons cheese. Put in broiler and heat until bubbly and lightly browned. Serve immediately. Makes 4.

MENU SUGGESTION: Blueberries (fresh or frozen and thawed) in honeydew wedge.

SOUFFLÉED CHEDDAR SANDWICH

3 eggs
½ teaspoon salt
½ teaspoon dry mustard
freshly ground black pepper
cayenne pepper to taste
1 cup grated or finely shredded Cheddar
**   cheese**
6 slices whole wheat bread or other
**   preferred bread**
softened butter or margarine

Preheat broiler. Separate eggs and beat yolks lightly. Add salt, mustard, black pepper, and cayenne pepper, and beat until thick and pale in color. Stir in Cheddar cheese. Beat the egg whites until soft peaks form and fold into the cheese mixture.

Arrange bread slices on baking sheet and toast one side in broiler. Remove from broiler, turn bread slices, and butter untoasted side. Arrange bread slices close together on baking sheet. Spoon the egg-cheese mixture evenly over bread slices. Bake 10–12 minutes in 350° oven, or until puffed and golden. Serve immediately.

Makes 6.

MENU SUGGESTION: Melon balls drizzled with honey.

EGGPLANT BACONWICH

1 eggplant
5 eggs
2 tablespoons milk
wheat germ or fine dry breadcrumbs
butter or margarine
4 slices bacon
4 or 8 slices Oatmeal Bread (bought or see
    Index) or similar bread

Wash eggplant but do not peel. Cut 4 large center slices of eggplant, about ⅜–½ inch thick. In a flat soup plate beat 1 egg lightly. Mix in the milk. Put wheat germ or breadcrumbs in another flat soup plate.

Melt 2 tablespoons butter in skillet. Dip eggplant slices in egg mixture, then in wheat germ, and sauté slowly on each side until nicely browned and tender. Set aside. Sauté bacon until nicely browned, drain on paper towels, and cut in half crosswise.

Meanwhile, toast 4 or 8 slices bread (depending on whether you want open or closed sandwiches). Butter the toast. Scramble the remaining eggs in a little of the bacon fat.

To assemble sandwiches, arrange a fried eggplant slice on each of the 4 slices of toast. Arrange ¼ of the scrambled eggs on each. Top with 2 of the bacon pieces. Eat open-faced with knife and fork or cover with buttered toast and cut sandwiches in half.

Makes 4.

MENU SUGGESTION: Clam-tomato juice or Bloody Marys.

MANDARIN CHICKEN SANDWICH CUPS

1 tablespoon sherry
4 teaspoons cornstarch
1 tablespoon soy sauce (preferably tamari
    soy sauce)
1 whole uncooked chicken breast, skinned,
    boned, and cut in slivers
1 scallion, including some of green part,
    sliced thin
8 slices soft white bread
butter or margarine
1½ cups chopped mushrooms
4 tablespoons vegetable oil
½ cup drained mandarin orange sections,
    cut in half crosswise
½ cup chicken broth
2 tablespoons slivered toasted almonds

Preheat oven at 400°. Combine sherry and corn-starch in a flat soup plate, stirring until smooth. Add soy sauce and stir again. Add chicken and scallion and toss all together, making sure chicken is well coated. Set aside.

Remove crusts from bread slices without removing any of the bread itself, if possible. Lightly butter 8 depressions of a muffin tin. Mold one slice of bread into each of the depressions, shaping with the fingers to form bread cups. If necessary, fill in any missing sections toward the top of the cups with other pieces of soft white bread. Put in oven for 3–5 minutes, until lightly browned. Remove from oven but leave toast cups in muffin tin.

In a skillet or wok, sauté mushrooms in 2 tablespoons oil until lightly browned. Add mandarin orange pieces and toss until heated. Remove with slotted spoon and put in a bowl. Add remaining oil to the skillet and heat slightly. Add the chicken mixture and stir-fry 3–4 minutes until chicken pieces have lost their color. Add chicken broth and cook, stirring, until thickened. Add mushroom-and-orange mixture and heat another minute.

Remove toast cups from muffin tin and place 2 on each serving plate. Spoon the chicken mixture equally into them. Sprinkle with almonds. Serve immediately.

Makes 4 servings.

MENU SUGGESTION: Make a big pot of China tea, such as Formosa Oolong or China Black, and serve with sugar, milk, or lemon as desired.

TIPSY SARDINES WITH MUSHROOMS
ON TOAST

4 tablespoons (approximately) butter or
   margarine
1/2 cup chopped onion
1 small garlic clove, minced
1 cup white wine
1 strip lemon peel
1 bay leaf
2 or 3 cans brisling sardines or any small
   unsmoked sardines or sprats which have
   not had skin and bones removed (total
   weight should be 6 1/2 –8 ounces)
1/4 pound sliced mushrooms (about 2 cups)
5 or 6 slices Four Grain Bread (see Index)
   or any preferred bread

Melt 1 tablespoon butter in small skillet and sauté onion and garlic until onion is soft. Add wine, lemon peel, and bay leaf. Bring to boil. Lower flame and simmer 10 minutes.

Meanwhile, drain sardines well and pat off oil with paper towels. Arrange in shallow soup dish. Strain wine mixture over sardines and allow to stand at room temperature 1–1 1/2 hours. Near end of marinating time sauté mushrooms in about 2 tablespoons butter until lightly browned. Toast bread and butter it.

Arrange 4 or 5 drained sardines on each piece of toast, discarding marinade. Spoon mushrooms over top. Makes 5 or 6 servings.

MENU SUGGESTION: Dried peaches, prunes, and pears which have been poached together with sugar and lemon slice and well chilled.

SAFFRON TOAST COTTAGE CHEESE SANDWICH

The pure and simple taste of fresh butter and cottage cheese allows the delicate flavor of the bread to dominate this sandwich.

1 loaf Saffron Bread (see Index)
softened sweet butter
creamed cottage cheese or whipped cream
   cheese

Slice bread reasonably thin. Toast and butter slices. Spread half the slices with cottage cheese or cream cheese. Put together and cut into halves or quarters. Or cut bread thickly and serve open-faced, cut into quarters.

A loaf will make about 9 closed sandwiches.

MENU SUGGESTION: Stewed strawberries and rhubarb to start. Café au lait with the sandwiches.

HUEVOS RANCHEROS ON TORTILLAS

1 4-ounce can taco sauce (such as Ashleys,
    Old El Paso, or Patio brand)
¼ cup water
½ teaspoon sugar
2 teaspoons vinegar
¼ teaspoon oregano
4 eggs
oil or lard for frying
4 corn tortillas (canned, packaged, or
    fresh)
4 teaspoons fresh or freeze-dried chopped
    cilantro (Chinese parsley) or flat parsley

Combine taco sauce, water, sugar, vinegar, and oregano in a skillet and bring to a simmer. Break eggs one at a time into a cup and slip into the hot sauce to poach. Meanwhile, heat about half an inch of oil or lard in a heavy skillet and fry tortillas one at a time until crisp, turning once. (Or cook according to package directions.) Tortillas should take only seconds on each side to cook. Drain on paper towels.

Put 1 tortilla on each serving plate. Place a poached egg on tortilla. Boil down sauce quickly if it is too thin, and spoon over eggs, dividing equally. Sprinkle with cilantro. Can be eaten with knife and fork or picked up and eaten with the hands.

Makes 4.

MENU SUGGESTION: Serve with refried beans and/or sliced avocado.

HAM WITH HEARTS OF PALM
BÉARNAISE SANDWICH

1 can hearts of palm
butter or margarine
thickly sliced ham, cut to fit bread slices
Béarnaise sauce (bought or homemade)
Danish light pumpernickel bread, or
**   similar bread**

Slice hearts of palm lengthwise into halves or thirds, depending on thickness of pieces, allowing 2 cut pieces per serving.

Melt 1 tablespoon butter in skillet and sauté ham slices until browned, allowing enough ham to cover 1 slice of bread for each serving. Turn and brown other side.

Meanwhile, heat Béarnaise sauce. Remove ham from skillet and sauté hearts of palm lightly on cut side(s), adding more butter to skillet if necessary.

Toast bread, allowing 1 slice for each serving. Butter toast. Arrange ham on toast. Arrange 2 pieces of hearts of palm on each serving, round sides up. Spoon a generous teaspoon Béarnaise sauce on each piece of heart of palm. Eat with knife and fork.

There are enough hearts of palm in 1 can for 8 servings.

MENU SUGGESTION: Apricot nectar.

ARNOLD'S BENEDICT SANDWICH

4 slices Canadian bacon
butter or margarine
4 eggs
4 English muffins (or crumpets for open-
    faced sandwiches)
½ cup béchamel sauce (see Index)
¼ cup or more grated Cheddar, Monterey
    Jack, or other flavorful cheese

Sauté Canadian bacon in 1 tablespoon butter lightly on both sides and set aside. Preheat broiler.

Heat enough water in a low pan or skillet for poaching eggs. Break eggs, one at a time, into a cup and slip into the hot water to poach.

Meanwhile, toast and butter English muffins. Arrange bottoms of muffins on a baking sheet. Put a slice of Canadian bacon on each. Put a drained poached egg on the Canadian bacon. Spoon 2 tablespoons béchamel sauce over each egg. Sprinkle each with 1 tablespoon or more grated cheese. Run under broiler until cheese and sauce are bubbly and lightly browned. Place on individual serving dishes with top half of muffins. Eat open-faced with knife and fork or close and eat with the hands.

Makes 4.

MENU SUGGESTION: Orange juice or Screwdrivers.

FROGS' LEGS ON PAPRIKA POINTS

6 pairs large frogs' legs (if frozen, thaw
   completely)
1 cup milk
½ cup water
½ cup finely chopped onion
½ small garlic clove, finely minced
4 or more tablespoons butter or margarine
½ cup flour
½ teaspoon salt
pepper to taste
1 or more tablespoons vegetable oil
½ cup white wine
½ teaspoon chervil
4 slices firm square white bread
2 or more tablespoons paprika
4 teaspoons finely chopped parsley

Place frogs' legs in a shallow flat ceramic, glass, or enamel pan or baking dish. Pour milk and water over them. Allow to sit in refrigerator 2 hours, turning once. Drain and dry thoroughly with paper towel.

Sauté onion and garlic in 1 tablespoon butter until onion is soft. Combine flour, salt, and pepper in a flat soup plate, and roll the frogs' legs in the mixture. Remove onions from skillet and set aside. Add about a tablespoon more butter and the oil to the skillet and sauté the frogs' legs, a few pairs at a time, until golden and cooked through, adding more butter and oil as necessary. When all have been sautéed and removed from the skillet, add wine to the skillet and heat, stirring, until all brown particles have been loosened from pan bottom. Turn off heat.

Remove meat from frogs' legs and discard bones and other inedible portions. Place skillet over gentle heat and add the sautéed onions and garlic, chervil, and the frog meat. Heat gently.

Meanwhile, butter bread on both sides and fry both sides over moderate heat. Sprinkle paprika evenly in a flat soup plate. When all bread slices have been fried, dip one side of each slice in the paprika. Place 1 slice, paprika side up, on each serving plate. Cut into quarters from corner to corner. Turn quarters around so they form a pinwheel pattern. Spoon the frog meat mixture into the center of each group of paprika triangles, dividing equally. Sprinkle a teaspoon of chopped parsley over each. Serve immediately.

Makes 4 servings.

MENU SUGGESTION: A champagne cocktail would not be amiss before this elegant brunch.

6. SANDWICHES FOR PICNIC TIME

And you're giving a treat (penny ice
and cold meat) to a party of friends
and relations—
They're a ravenous horde—and they
all come on board at Sloane Square
and South Kensington Stations.
—W. S. GILBERT, *Iolanthe*

Off to the seashore, the lakeside, or a bosky dell in the
woods on a fine summer's day with a hamper of sandwiches and some cool drinks. This can be one of life's
finer moments—with the right company, of course, and
the right sandwiches. Picnic sandwiches, apart from
other sandwiches, must be especially refreshing, ca-
pable of being transported without deteriorating, and
very tasteful, since they're eaten outdoors, where appetites and taste buds seem somehow at their sharpest.
The sandwiches in this chapter fill the bill on all scores,

and the selection is diverse enough for the simplest menu or the most festive of get-togethers.

We can thank the French for the idea of the picnic, and for making up the word *piquenique* in the seventeenth century to describe the event. We can thank American ingenuity for the manufacture of the thermal carrier and ice chest that make it possible now for us to carry all our picnic delights without fear of finding spoiled or soggy food on arrival. Remember to pack moist fillings, salad greens, and similar types of foods separately in plastic bags or containers, and to keep them well chilled until you're ready to eat. The sandwiches in this chapter are made without lettuce, but if you feel it must be included, slip it into the sandwiches at the last possible moment before serving.

Carry along paper plates and napkins, knives, forks, and spoons if needed, unbreakable glasses, salt and pepper, and the always-needed bottle or can opener and corkscrew. Add to that a large knife for cutting long loaves into wedges and a big spoon for scooping out salads and fillings, and you have all you need to make your picnic paraphernalia complete. You may need a thermal bucket of ice, depending on what you've chosen to drink, and don't forget to take along a trash bag for your litter.

You'll find suggestions for making your picnic menu complete at the end of the recipes.

EUROPEAN WORKMEN'S SANDWICHES

It's almost effortless to make up a batch of these earthy and satisfying sandwiches, and the combinations are seemingly endless. The sandwiches are all made up of cheese and sausage or cured meat, sliced and tucked into wedges of French or Italian bread. Don't butter the bread, and free yourself from carrying thermal equipment. Simply cut the bread into 5- or 6-inch lengths, slit open and fill with whichever cheese-sausage combo appeals to you from the list below, wrap in aluminum foil, and pack in a basket. Be sure to take along a pot of good mustard and an assortment of pickles—for example, big dills, little gherkins, senf-gurken, mustard pickles, yellow dill cherries, any of the pickles in Chapter 8, or any other favorites or unusual kinds you happen to find.

Cheese and Sausage Combinations

Danish Havarti	Polish kielbasy
Norwegian Jarlsberg	Lebanon bologna
Muenster or Tilsit	German cervelat
Appenzell or Gruyère	Braunschweiger liver sausage
Italian Fontina	Italian soft salami
Spanish Manchego	chorizo
Danbo	Danish smoked salami
French Port Salut	Hungarian salami
Holland Gouda	Black Forest smoked pork
Leyden or Nokkelost, or other seeded cheese	Italian hard salami

MENU SUGGESTION: A jug of red wine and a basket of fresh fruit.

BIG RAW VEGETABLE PILLOWS

1 cup sliced mushrooms
1 cup shredded carrots
½ cup chopped green pepper
½ cup chopped pimientos
1 cup shredded red cabbage
1 cup fresh bean sprouts or drained canned
    bean sprouts
1 cup thinly sliced zucchini
1 cup plain yogurt
4 scallions, including some of green part,
    finely chopped
½ teaspoon celery salt
2 tablespoons chopped parsley
½ teaspoon salt, or to taste
freshly ground pepper to taste
1 teaspoon chopped fresh dill or ½ teaspoon
    dill weed
6 to 8 pita breads, either whole wheat or white
    (bought or see Index)

Toss mushrooms, carrots, green pepper, pimientos, cabbage, bean sprouts, and zucchini together and pack in covered plastic container. Combine yogurt, scallions, celery salt, parsley, salt, pepper, and dill, and spoon into another covered plastic container. Pack both containers, along with pita bread wrapped in plastic wrap, in ice chest or thermal carrier.

At picnic site pour yogurt mixture over vegetables and toss. Slit open pita breads about ⅓ of the way around the edge. Fill with vegetable mixture, dividing equally.

Makes 6–8, depending on size of pita breads.

MENU SUGGESTION: A thermos of hot avgolemono (Greek lemon, egg, and chicken broth soup), or chilled consommé madrilène.

HOLY MACKEREL SANDWICH

4 or 6 slices Cheddar Bread (see Index) or
   other cheese bread
softened butter or margarine
1 can fillet of mackerel in white wine or
   vinaigrette
green cracked olives, sliced lengthwise, pits
   removed

Toast bread and butter it. Drain the fillet of mackerel very well. Arrange the fillets on half of the toast slices. Cover with olive slices, allowing 2 olives per sandwich if the olives are large. Cover with remaining toast slices. Cut in half, wrap individually in plastic wrap, and transport in ice chest or thermal carrier.

Makes 2 or 3.

MENU SUGGESTION: Robert's Shredded Raw Carrots Vinaigrette (see Index), or your own version.

FIVE FRUIT AND NUT BREAD SANDWICHES

On a hot summer's day when meats and heavy foods seem out of order, have a refreshing picnic of sandwiches made from fruit or nut bread and simple but good-tasting fillings. Have one kind or several. The breads can all be made days ahead and refrigerated, or weeks ahead and kept on hand in the freezer. Or substitute homemade fruit and nut breads you come upon in bakeries, health-food stores, farmers' markets, roadside stands, specialty food shops, and so on.

No. 1. Zippy Edam Sandwich

Pecan Bread (see Index) or similar bought
   bread
softened butter or margarine
grated Edam cheese, firmly packed (¼ cup
   per sandwich)
lemon juice (1 teaspoon per sandwich)
curry powder (¼ teaspoon per sandwich)

Slice bread thinly and butter it. Combine Edam, lemon juice, and curry powder and use for sandwich filling. Close, cut in half, wrap individually in plastic wrap, and transport in thermal carrier or ice chest.

No. 2. Ginger Pumpkin Sandwich

**Pumpkin Bread (see Index) or similar bought
  bread
softened butter or margarine
1 3-ounce package cream cheese
1 or more tablespoons milk or cream
1 teaspoon finely chopped crystallized ginger**

Slice bread thinly and butter it. Cream the cream cheese and add enough milk or cream to make of proper spreading consistency. Mix in the ginger. Spread as thickly as you like on bread. Close, cut in half, wrap individually in plastic wrap, and transport in thermal carrier or ice chest.

No. 3. Peanut Butter Lemon Marmalade Banana Bread Sandwich

**Banana Bread (see Index)
softened butter or margarine
peanut butter (preferably 100-percent-
  peanuts type)
lemon or lime marmalade**

Slice bread thinly and butter it. Make sandwiches, spreading bread first with peanut butter, then marmalade. Close sandwiches, cut in half, wrap individually in plastic wrap, and transport in thermal carrier or ice chest.

No. 4. Vitamin C Sandwich

Orange Sunflower Bread (see Index) or
**   similar bought bread**
softened butter or margarine
rosehip jam

Slice bread thinly and butter it. Spread bread thickly with rosehip jam. Close sandwiches, cut in half, wrap individually in plastic wrap, and transport in thermal carrier or ice chest.

No. 5. Apple-Date-Chestnut Sandwich

Apple Honey Date Bread (see Index) or
**   similar bought bread**
softened butter or margarine
1 small can sweetened chestnut spread (crème
**   de marrons, available at specialty food**
**   stores and in some grocery stores and**
**   supermarkets)**
instant dry milk powder, optional

Slice bread thinly and butter it. Make sandwiches with chestnut spread. (In the unlikely event that the chestnut spread is too thin to spread properly, add instant dry milk powder, mixing thoroughly, until of proper spreading consistency.) Close sandwiches, cut in half, wrap individually in plastic wrap, and transport in thermal carrier or ice chest.

MENU SUGGESTION: Pack some ice-cold ginger ale and a big bag of fresh dark cherries to go with any or all of these sandwiches.

BREADSTICK SANDWICHES

These sandwiches are built in reverse order—the filling is on the outside and the bread hides in the center. Sauces go along for dipping. They're fun to eat and easy to make up and carry.

6 very thin slices prosciutto ham
6 very thin large slices rare roast beef
6 very thin large slices Jarlsberg or Swiss cheese
18 short thick Italian sesame breadsticks
¾ cup mayonnaise
2 or 3 tablespoons Dijon mustard or any well-flavored mustard
horseradish dressing (see Index, or use bottled horseradish dressing)

Lay out the slices of meat and cheese. Place a breadstick at the end of each slice and roll up, folding in sides if necessary, to make a neat rolled-up sandwich. When all are rolled up make aluminum-foil bundles, each containing a stick of prosciutto, roast beef, and cheese. Combine mayonnaise and mustard and spoon into covered plastic jar. Spoon horseradish dressing into another covered plastic jar. Pack all in ice chest or thermal carrier, and include plastic spoons and plates so that each person can spoon some sauce onto his plate and dip the breadsticks in at will. Makes 6 servings.

MENU SUGGESTION: A green-bean-and-bacon salad with oil-and-vinegar dressing. If you aren't going to be traveling too far before eating, take along a plastic container filled with your favorite flavor Italian ice. Put it in an ice-cream bag or wrap in many layers of newspaper and pack it in the ice chest or thermal carrier.

PAN BAGNAT

There are no set proportions for this popular Riviera sandwich. Use as much or as little of each ingredient as you like, or substitute other ingredients such as chicken, sausage, bacon, or ratatouille as you see fit.

**4 round hard rolls or French rolls, or 2
    10- to 12-inch loaves French or Italian bread
olive oil
1 garlic clove
1 large ripe tomato, thinly sliced
green pepper strips
black olives, pits removed (dry oil-cured
    olives, or Italian, Greek, or niçoise olives.
    If using oil-cured olives, make sure they
    have not been sprinkled with red pepper
    flakes.)
red Italian onion, thinly sliced
2 hard-cooked eggs, sliced
1 or 2 cans tuna fillets, or 1 6½-ounce can
    tuna
radishes, thinly sliced
flat anchovies
red wine vinegar
freshly ground pepper**

Cut rolls or bread in half horizontally, pull out some of soft part, and set aside for another use. Brush inside of bread with oil. Rub cut garlic over the oil. Arrange tomato slices on bottom half of bread. Cover with a layer of green pepper, olives, onion, egg slices, and tuna. Sprinkle a few radish slices on the tuna and arrange some anchovies on top. Sprinkle vinegar over top and finish with a few grinds of pepper. Close the bread, press down with your hands, and wrap each roll in aluminum foil. Weight down with some heavy object for half an hour. Remove weight and refrigerate until ready to transport in ice chest or thermal carrier. If using French or Italian bread, cut the Pan Bagnat in half.

Makes 4 servings.

MENU SUGGESTION: Chilled white wine is ideal. Otherwise, a big thermos of lemonade.

SESAME PEANUT BUTTER SUNSHINE SANDWICH

peanut butter (preferably 100-percent-
   peanuts type)
tahini (ground sesame seed)
Dark Soy-Carob Bread (see Index) or other
   dark bread
banana
lemon juice
sunflower seeds

Combine equal parts peanut butter and tahini. Spread thickly on bread slices. Peel banana and cut diagonally into ¼-inch slices. Brush with lemon juice. Arrange several banana slices on half the bread slices. Sprinkle generously with sunflower seeds. Cover with remaining bread slices. Cut in half and wrap in aluminum foil.

MENU SUGGESTION: Pack your sandwiches in an ice chest or thermal carrier, along with a thermos or two of ice-cold borscht shaken up with some sour cream, which will be a beautiful pink color and refreshingly cool.

GALA PICNIC SANDWICH À LA RUSSE

1 cup cooked diced carrots

1 cup cooked fresh or frozen small green peas

1 cup cooked fresh or frozen cauliflower
   florets

1 cup cooked green beans, cut crosswise in
   ¾-inch lengths

2 cups diced cooked chicken, preferably
   white meat

1 cup diced cooked veal (you can use ¼ pound
   veal scaloppine which has been sautéed
   quickly in a little butter and oil on both
   sides, then diced)

2 cups diced ham

1 cup diced lobster meat

10 tablespoons vinaigrette dressing (see
   Index)

1 cup diced celery

1 cup peeled, seeded, diced cucumber

¼ cup finely sliced scallions, including some
   of green part

1 cup diced dill pickle

6 flat anchovy fillets, cut into small pieces

¼ cup drained capers

½ cup pimiento strips

1 cup mayonnaise

1 round loaf Italian bread 15–16 inches in
   diameter, or 3 round loaves Italian bread
   7½–8 inches in diameter (the large loaf
   can be ordered from some Italian bakeries)

softened butter or margarine

The carrots, peas, cauliflower, and green beans should be cooked separately until just crisp tender. Put each of them, drained, in a separate small bowl or glass jar. Also put the chicken, veal, ham, and lobster in separate bowls or glass jars. Pour 1 tablespoon vinaigrette dressing over each, plus an extra tablespoon each for the chicken and ham. Toss lightly. Cover and refrigerate 6 hours or overnight, turning once or twice.

Combine celery, cucumber, scallions, pickle, anchovies, capers, and pimiento strips in a large bowl. Add all of the refrigerated vegetables and meats and their dressings. Toss lightly. Add mayonnaise and toss again, gently. Pack into a 3- or 4-quart covered plastic container and put in ice chest.

Cut top off bread. Cut around sides of bread about 1/2 inch from edge. Pull out inside of bread, leaving a 1/2-inch shell all around. (Reserve the soft part of bread for another use.) Butter inside and cut side of top of bread. Replace top. Wrap bread in aluminum foil and pack in ice chest. At picnic site fill shell with the vegetable-meat combination, mounding over top. Set top on. To serve, slice as you would a pie. It is easier to cut with the lid removed.

Makes 12 servings.

MENU SUGGESTION: This festive sandwich calls for a bottle or two of champagne. Nestle them in ice cubes in an ice chest so they stay deliciously cold.

TUNA TOTES

½ stick butter or margarine
1 teaspoon anchovy paste
½ teaspoon lemon juice
½ teaspoon paprika
4 large hard whole wheat rolls (bought, or see
Index: Crusty Whole Wheat Hamburger
Rolls), or hard white rolls
2 6½-ounce cans chunk tuna, drained
2 large ripe tomatoes, thickly sliced
1 cup shredded Cheddar cheese, or any
preferred cheese
sesame seeds

Cream the butter until soft. Add anchovy paste, lemon juice, and paprika and blend well. Cut rolls open, pull out soft part, and reserve for another use. Spread insides of rolls with butter-anchovy mixture. Arrange half a can of tuna in each roll. Cover with tomato slices. Cover with shredded cheese, pressing down lightly with hand and making sure tomato is entirely covered. Sprinkle generously with sesame seeds. Close sandwiches and wrap individually in aluminum foil. Transport in ice chest or thermal carrier.

Makes 4.

MENU SUGGESTION: German potato salad.

THE HERO

Here is a hero fit for a king. Feel free to add or subtract filling ingredients to your taste, or change quantities to suit your capacity—but you can't go wrong with the combination below.

> 1 loaf Italian bread
> olive oil
> 1 garlic clove
> 1/4 pound Gorgonzola cheese at room
>   temperature
> 1/4 pound each of 4 or more of the following
>   meats: Genoa salami, prosciutto, morta-
>   della, capicola, pepperoni
> 1/4–1/2 pound provolone or Taleggio cheese
> 6 or more pepperoncini (Tuscan peppers)
> 2 or 3 roasted sweet peppers
> a few flat anchovies
> small hot peppers to taste (optional)
> vinegar

Cut bread open lengthwise. Brush cut sides with oil. Rub cut garlic clove over oil. Spread the bottom half of bread thinly with Gorgonzola. Arrange layers of meat over it. Cover with a layer of provolone or Taleggio cheese. Cover with pepperoncini and/or roasted sweet peppers, anchovies, and a few hot peppers if desired. Sprinkle lightly with vinegar. Cover with top of bread and wrap tightly in aluminum foil. At picnic site cut into 4 portions. Makes 4 servings.

MENU SUGGESTION: For a spring or fall picnic carry along a thermos of piping-hot minestrone.

The Endless Hero: You can fool your friends, save a lot of money compared with delicatessen prices for similar gigantic heros, and have a marvelous time making a three-foot long, six-foot long, or any other length sandwich without having to find a loaf of bread of extraordinary length. You will also have an extraordinary picnic. Here's how you do it.

First decide on the length of your finished hero, allowing 4 servings from each ordinary-size loaf of Italian bread used. Then get a plank the same length. You'll be limited only by the size of the car, station wagon, van, or trailer truck in which you'll be transporting your hero. Cover the plank with aluminum foil. Then buy as many loaves of Italian bread as you will need to cover the plank after you have cut about 3 inches off the ends of each loaf so that all the bread will be of uniform width. Then proceed to make your hero as above, cut it into wedges, and line the wedges up on the plank, fitting them closely together so they look as if they started out as one giant loaf. Cover bread with plastic wrap, tucking in underneath to keep filling in place. Then cover the entire sandwich and plank with aluminum foil and head for the hills.

FRUITARIAN SANDWICHES

These are for people who are tired of meat and refuse to eat vegetables.

> 1 cup crushed pineapple (preferably
> unsweetened), drained
> 1 large banana, sliced
> ½ cup mandarin orange segments cut in half
> crosswise, or cut-up fresh oranges
> 1 cup seedless grapes, cut in half crosswise
> 1 mango or 2 ripe peaches, peeled and cut
> into small pieces
> 1 hard red apple, cored and cut into small
> pieces
> 3 cups cottage cheese
> 16 slices (1 loaf) Irish Seedy Bread (see Index)
> softened butter or margarine

Combine all fruits, tossing lightly. Add cottage cheese and mix gently but thoroughly. Pack in covered plastic container. Toast bread and butter it. Wrap in aluminum foil. Pack all in ice chest or thermal carrier.

At picnic site pile fruit-cheese mixture onto bread. Close sandwiches and cut in half (or make the sandwiches open-faced).

Makes 8 closed sandwiches.

MENU SUGGESTION: Depending on weather, personal preference, age, and mood, a big thermos of chocolate milk or hot chocolate. Spice cupcakes with fluffy white frosting would end this picnic nicely.

STARS AND STRIPES

Striped sandwiches are picnic classics, but scrumptious fillings make these out of the ordinary. The stars (other than you and your guests, of course) are pickle slices cut into star shapes with a small cookie cutter, which you might like to serve along with the sandwiches, particularly for a Fourth of July picnic.

1 cucumber
salt
1 loaf unsliced wheat germ or cracked wheat bread
1 loaf unsliced pumpernickel or other dark bread
1 loaf unsliced firm white bread
1½ sticks butter or margarine, at room temperature
3 tablespoons grated Parmesan, Romano, or Sardo cheese
freshly ground pepper to taste
2 tablespoons capers, minced
1 teaspoon grated onion
1 tablespoon fine dry breadcrumbs
2 ounces cream cheese
3 tablespoons finely chopped pimiento-stuffed olives
1 bunch watercress (1 cup or more leaves)
1 bunch (7 medium-size) radishes, trimmed and thinly sliced
large pickle slices cut into stars with star-shaped cookie cutter (optional)

Peel cucumber and cut in half lengthwise. Remove seeds. Slice thinly, sprinkle with salt, and place in colander to drain for about 30 minutes. Pat dry with paper towel.

Meanwhile, cut bottom crusts off the 3 loaves of bread. Cut 2 horizontal slices about ⅓ inch thick from each of the dark loaves and 1 slice about ⅓ inch thick from the white loaf. (Reserve remaining bread for another use.) Stack up bread slices and trim off all remaining crusts evenly.

Cream ½ stick butter and mix in the grated cheese and pepper until well blended. Cream ½ stick butter and blend in the capers, onion, and breadcrumbs. Cream remaining butter with the cream cheese. Add olives and mix until well blended.

Wash watercress, remove leaves, and discard stems. Dry leaves well.

Place 1 pumpernickel slice on a large sheet of heavy-duty aluminum foil and spread with half the cheese butter. Arrange a double layer of radish slices on top. Spread one of the wheat germ or cracked wheat slices with ⅓ of the olive butter, and put buttered side down on the radishes. Spread top with ½ of the caper butter. Arrange cucumber slices on top. Spread one side of the white bread slice with another ⅓ of the olive butter and lay on top of the sandwich, buttered side down. Spread remaining pumpernickel slice with remaining half of cheese butter and lay on sandwich, buttered side down. Spread top with remaining caper butter. Arrange watercress leaves on top. Spread remaining wheat germ or cracked wheat slice with remaining olive butter and lay on sandwich, buttered side down. Bring foil up around sandwich loaf and seal tightly all around. Chill in refrigerator or ice chest at least 8 hours before eating. Pack pickle slices in a covered plastic container.

At picnic site unwrap sandwich loaf and slice into ¾-inch slices.

Makes 10–12 servings, depending on length of the shortest loaf of bread used to make the sandwich loaf.

MENU SUGGESTION: If you don't think these sandwiches will fill you up, pack some cold fried chicken legs in your ice chest or thermal carrier.

NUTTY SEEDY SANDWICHES

Make either or both of the following nut spreads for great meatless sandwiches to tote along on a picnic. No thermal equipment is needed if you want to travel light, but a thermal carrier will keep the sandwiches cooler, of course, and allow you to butter the bread. You can then take along a salad and cold drinks, too.

> **Herb Bread (see Index) or other whole-grain bread**
> **softened butter or margarine (optional)**
> **Cashew Butter and/or Peanut Soy Butter (recipes follow)**

Cashew Butter

> **½ cup sesame seeds**
> **½ cup sunflower seeds**
> **1 cup cashew nuts, salted or unsalted**
> **1 tablespoon honey**
> **3–4 tablespoons vegetable oil**
> **salt to taste**

Place seeds in food processor or blender and process until pulverized. Add nuts and process again until pulverized, stopping to scrape down sides of container if necessary. Add honey and 1 tablespoon of oil and blend again. Add salt if desired. Add more oil, 1 tablespoon at a time, blending after each addition, until cashew butter is smooth and spreadable. Store in tightly sealed glass jar.

Peanut Soy Butter

1 cup cooked drained soybeans
1 cup roasted shelled peanuts, salted or
   unsalted
2 or more tablespoons vegetable oil
1 tablespoon chopped chives
1 teaspoon salt

Place soy beans and peanuts in blender or food
processor and blend until fine, stopping to scrape down
sides of container if necessary. Add oil 1 tablespoon at
a time, blending after each addition, until of proper
spreading consistency. Add chives and salt and blend
again. Add more salt if desired. Store in tightly sealed
glass jar.

MENU SUGGESTION: Shredded Beet Salad (see Index, or use
your own favorite recipe).

THREE SPECIAL MEAT SANDWICHES

Each of these sandwiches is a special treat and out-of-the-ordinary picnic fare. The smoked turkey breast and Westphalian ham can be bought by the slice in certain meat stores, delicatessens, and ethnic-food markets. The Chinese roast pork you make yourself when you feel adventurous and want to try a cooking method you've probably never tried before.

Sandwich No. 1. Smoked Turkey Breast on Tomato Bread

> Tomato Bread (see Index) or any preferred
>   bread
> softened butter or margarine
> sliced smoked turkey breast (2 ounces per
>   sandwich)
> Russian dressing (see Index)
> Boston lettuce or other buttery-type lettuce
>   (optional)

Slice the bread and butter 2 slices per sandwich. Arrange smoked turkey breast slices on bread and spread thickly with Russian dressing. Arrange lettuce leaves over dressing if desired. Close and cut sandwich in half. Wrap tightly in plastic wrap. Transport in thermal carrier or ice chest.

MENU SUGGESTION: White Salad (see Index). Omit the endive and carry the salad in a plastic container in the thermal carrier or ice chest.

Sandwich No. 2. Open-faced Westphalian Sandwich

softened sweet butter
2 slices Westphalian pumpernickel, or similar
   pumpernickel
1 hard-cooked egg
1 tablespoon mayonnaise
½ teaspoon Dijon mustard
freshly ground pepper to taste
4 thin slices Westphalian ham (about 1½
   ounces)

Butter the bread. Chop the egg and combine with mayonnaise, mustard, and pepper. Spread over both slices of bread. Arrange 2 slices Westphalian ham over each sandwich. Cut in half. Wrap each sandwich tightly in plastic wrap. Transport in thermal carrier or ice chest.

Makes 2.

MENU SUGGESTION: Pickled red cabbage, chilled and served as a salad, and well-chilled beer (Westphalian beer if you can find some).

Sandwich No. 3. Chinese Roast Pork Sandwich with Scallion Dressing

> 1 boneless fresh pork tenderloin (a long narrow strip of meat that weighs 1–1¼ pounds)
> 3 tablespoons sherry
> ½ teaspoon salt
> 2 tablespoons soy sauce (preferably tamari soy sauce)
> 1 tablespoon honey
> 1 garlic clove, minced
> 4 slices fresh ginger root or canned green ginger root, minced
> 1 scallion, including some of green part, finely chopped
> 2 tablespoons Hoisin sauce
> 12 slices firm white bread
> softened butter or margarine

For the scallion dressing:
> 4 scallions, thinly sliced and separated into rings
> 3 tablespoons soy sauce (preferably tamari soy sauce)
> 3 tablespoons white vinegar or rice vinegar
> 4 teaspoons sugar
> ½ teaspoon five spices powder*

---

* Five spices powder can be found in Oriental stores, specialty food stores, and on spice racks in certain supermarkets. If it is not available, you can substitute a pinch or so each of ground anise seed, cloves, ginger, and nutmeg, using more of the anise seed than the other spices.

Cut pork into 4-inch lengths and cut each of these in half lengthwise. Arrange in a shallow ceramic, glass, or enameled pan or baking dish. Combine sherry, salt, soy sauce, honey, garlic, ginger, scallion, and Hoisin sauce, and pour over the meat. Cover and marinate in refrigerator 1–1½ hours, turning several times.

Meanwhile, prepare oven for roasting. Set one shelf on the lowest slot and place a large shallow pan of hot water on it. Make 6 S-shaped hooks of steel wire or giant-size paper clips. Set another oven shelf on the highest slot in the oven. You will be putting a hook through the top of each piece of meat and hanging it from the top rack. The pan of water will be underneath to catch drips and provide steam for keeping the meat moist. Make certain that there is enough space between the two shelves so that the meat does not touch the water in the pan. You can hang the meat higher if necessary by putting the hooks through the meat closer to the center rather than at the top.

Preheat oven at 350°. Hang meat from top rack and roast 35 minutes. While meat is roasting, prepare scallion dressing as follows. Combine scallions, soy sauce, vinegar, sugar, and five spices powder in a small bowl. Cover and set aside.

After meat has roasted 35 minutes raise oven temperature to 450° and roast another 10–15 minutes. Watch carefully and do not allow the meat to burn. The narrower strips may need to be removed from the oven before the thicker ones. Using potholders, remove hooks from meat and allow to cool. Cut crosswise into thin slices.

Toast bread and butter it. Arrange a single layer of pork slices on half of the toast slices. With a slotted spoon remove scallions from dressing and, dividing equally, arrange them over the pork. Close the sandwiches and cut in half. Wrap tightly, individually, in plastic wrap or aluminum foil and transport in ice chest or thermal carrier.

Pour remaining scallion dressing into a jar, cap tightly, and carry along to serve with the sandwiches. At serving time spoon some over each sandwich or let each person do his according to taste.

Note: This is also a great sandwich to serve hot when you aren't going on a picnic. Slice the meat as soon as it comes from the oven, make the sandwiches, and serve immediately.

Makes 6.

MENU SUGGESTION: Take along a container filled with a mixture of pineapple chunks, mandarin orange segments, lichees, and/or guava shells. Don't forget the fortune cookies.

7. SANDWICHES FOR COOKOUT TIME

Setting out well is a quarter of the journey.
—H. G. Bohn, *Handbook of Proverbs* (1855)

Whether you have a portable stove and tote it along on a day's outing, or have a more permanent kind of cookout equipment on your patio or in your back yard, it's not the type or location of the stove but what you cook on it that makes your cookouts memorable. In this chapter you'll find enough flavorsome cookout sandwich ideas to keep your kettle cooker, hibachi, gas grill, or outdoor fireplace busy for many a day to come.

Build your fire according to manufacturer's instructions or according to your woodsman's instinct, but if you can, avoid the use of fire starters that make food taste of kerosene or strange unwanted chemicals. Most of the sandwiches in this chapter are arranged in basket-type hand grills which are set over the fire and are easy to turn. Use long tongs, in preference to a long fork, to turn other sandwiches and foods cooked over the fire. Keep good thick potholders handy so you'll have them when you need them. Baking sheets make handy trays to use around cookout fires, since you can set hot things on them without fear of breakage, burning, or staining. With each cookout sandwich recipe you'll find a suggested accompaniment or two to complement the sandwich you're making.

CURRIED SHRIMP IN CRISP COCONUT ROLLS

¼ cup vegetable oil
¼ cup lemon juice
1 tablespoon curry powder
1 teaspoon ground ginger
1 teaspoon chopped mint
1 garlic clove, crushed
20 large or 28 medium shrimp, shelled and
    deveined
4 hot dog rolls
½ stick butter or margarine
¼ cup unsweetened coconut, finely chopped

Combine oil, lemon juice, curry powder, ginger, mint, and garlic in a bowl and toss with shrimp. Cover and refrigerate 8 hours, turning several times. Drain shrimp and put on 4 skewers.

Open hot dog rolls without separating halves. Cream butter until soft. Add coconut and mix well. Spread insides of rolls with coconut mixture. Set aside.

Grill shrimp over fire several minutes, turning the skewers and taking care not to overcook. Remove from fire. Toast rolls, coconut side down, until browned. Remove from fire. Remove shrimp from skewers and arrange a skewerful of shrimp in each roll. Serve immediately.

Makes 4.

MENU SUGGESTION: Corn on the cob.

NORWEGIAN MEATBALL SANDWICH

1 tablespoon butter or margarine
½ cup chopped onion
1 egg
½ cup milk
1 slice soft white bread, shredded into
    crumbs
2 teaspoons sugar
1¼ teaspoons salt
½ teaspoon nutmeg
¼ teaspoon allspice
1 pound ground beef
¼ pound ground lean pork
2 loaves French or Italian bread
softened butter or margarine

For the sauce:
2 medium onions, sliced
2 tablespoons butter or margarine
½ teaspoon salt
freshly ground pepper to taste
pinch of allspice
½ cup sour cream

Heat butter in a skillet and sauté onion until soft and slightly browned. Set aside. Beat egg in a large bowl. Add milk and combine. Add breadcrumbs, sugar, salt, nutmeg, and allspice, and mix well. Add the onion and mix well. Add ground beef and pork and mix until thoroughly combined. Divide mixture into 4 equal parts and shape 12 meatballs from each, for a total of 48 meatballs about 1 inch in diameter. Arrange in a single layer on 1 or 2 plates or large, flat platter. Cover with plastic wrap and refrigerate 1 hour or longer.

Begin the sauce by sautéing onions in butter in a skillet over the fire until lightly browned and soft. Add salt, pepper, and allspice, and set on back of grill to keep warm.

Put meatballs in oiled basket-type hand grill and brown slowly over fire on all sides until well done. Remove from fire.

Cut bread in half lengthwise. Remove some of soft inner part and toast cut sides over fire. Butter the toasted sides.

Stir sour cream into sauce mixture and remove from fire. Arrange 24 meatballs in each loaf of bread and top with half the onion–sour cream sauce. Close sandwiches and cut each into 3 wedges. Serve immediately.

Makes 6 servings.

MENU SUGGESTION: Peter Piper's Fresh Green Pickled Peppers (see Index).

TARRAGON TUNA TUCK-INS

1 8-ounce package refrigerated crescent
   dinner rolls
1 6½-ounce can chunk or flake tuna, well
   drained
½ teaspoon tarragon
¼ teaspoon salt
freshly ground pepper to taste
2–3 tablespoons mayonnaise
melted butter or margarine, or vegetable oil

Open package of rolls and, on a floured board, lay
out in sets of two triangles together to form squares.
You will have four squares. Roll each square out into a
5" x 6" rectangle.

Combine tuna, tarragon, salt, pepper, and enough
mayonnaise to hold the mixture together. Spoon onto
right sides of the squares, dividing equally. Fold the left
side over the filling so the edges meet. Seal the three
open sides of each rectangle and press with tines of a
fork. Brush all over with butter or oil. With a spatula,
transfer to an oiled basket-type hand grill. Heat slowly,
turning, over a low fire about 15 minutes until puffed
and nicely browned on both sides. Serve immediately.
   Makes 4.

MENU SUGGESTION: Mustard-deviled eggs.

CHALUPAS

Besides a fire, you'll need a small skillet, a medium-size saucepan, a little patience in stirring the beans, a quick hand at getting the tortillas in and out of the hot oil, and a good appetite to demolish the dozen chalupas you turn out. Don't forget paper napkins for the inevitable spillovers when eating.

2 1-pound cans refried beans
1 small bottle or can of beer
vegetable oil
12 corn tortillas, canned, packaged, or fresh
½ head iceberg lettuce, shredded
2 or 3 medium-size tomatoes, chopped
**¼ pound Cheddar, brick, or similar cheese,
    shredded**
**1 small can Mexican hot sauce or taco sauce
    (such as Rotel, Patio, Ashleys, or Old El
    Paso brand)**

Empty refried beans into saucepan and heat slowly, adding beer as necessary and stirring often, until beans are consistency of soft mashed potatoes.

Meanwhile, heat ¼–½ inch oil in skillet. Fry tortillas quickly, one at a time, in the hot oil, turning once and making sure tortilla is immersed in the oil on each side. It takes only a few seconds on each side until tortillas are crisp. Drain on paper towels.

When beans are heated through, spread over tortillas and top with a mound of lettuce and a spoonful each of tomato and cheese. Let each person put his own hot sauce on top according to taste. Makes 12.

MENU SUGGESTION: Cream of corn soup before the chalupas, and ice-cold beer with them.

ROQUEFORT STEAK SANDWICHES

2 ounces Roquefort cheese at room
   temperature
4½ tablespoons or more softened butter or
   margarine
½ tablespoon grated onion
1 tablespoon lemon juice
½ teaspoon Worcestershire sauce
dash of Tabasco sauce
4 club steaks ½–¾ inch thick
8 thick slices Danish light pumpernickel or
   similar bread

Break up Roquefort cheese with a fork. Add 1½ tablespoons butter and cream mixture until soft and smooth. Add onion, lemon juice, Worcestershire sauce, and Tabasco sauce, and blend well. Spread evenly on both sides of steaks. Pile steaks one atop another and wrap in aluminum foil. Refrigerate 6–10 hours.

Remove steaks from refrigerator 1 hour before ready to cook them. Arrange in oiled hand grill and grill over fire a few minutes on each side, taking care not to overcook. Steaks are thin and will cook quickly. While steaks are grilling, toast bread over fire on both sides. Spread toast with remaining butter and sandwich the steaks between slices. Cut sandwiches in half and serve immediately.

Makes 4 servings.

MENU SUGGESTION: Grilled tomatoes and potato chips.

SOLE SANDWICHES OVER FENNEL FIRE

There's fennel seed in the sole marinade, but for an extra nice touch of the herb drop some fennel twigs into your fire just before you start to grill the fish. Fennel twigs are sold boxed in most stores carrying herbs and spices.

> ⅓ cup lime or lemon juice
> 1½ teaspoons fennel seed
> 2 tablespoons brandy
> 1 pound fillet of sole or flounder
> ½ stick butter or margarine
> Boston lettuce or other buttery-type lettuce
> 1 loaf whole wheat Italian bread (see Index)
>   or white Italian bread
> tartar sauce (see Index)

Combine lime or lemon juice, fennel seed, and brandy in a shallow glass, ceramic, or enamel pan. Add the fillet and turn so both sides are coated. Cover, refrigerate, and allow to marinate 1–1½ hours, turning once or twice.

Remove fillets from marinade and dry with paper towel. Melt butter in small saucepan over fire. Brush over fillets. Place fillets in oiled hand grill. Add leftover marinade to melted butter remaining in saucepan and put over fire to boil down. Grill fillets a few minutes on each side, brushing with the butter mixture. Take care not to overcook the fish.

Meanwhile, cut bread in half lengthwise. Brush with butter mixture and toast cut sides over fire. When fish and bread have been removed from fire, arrange the fillets on the bottom half of bread, and pour the reduced sauce over them and over the cut side of the top of the bread. Arrange lettuce over the fillets. Close the loaf of bread and cut into 6–8 wedges. Serve immediately with tartar sauce.

Makes 6–8 wedges.

MENU SUGGESTION: French fries, which can also be dipped in the tartar sauce.

FIVE SANDWICHES FOR OUTDOOR GRILLING

The fillings for these sandwiches are prepared in the kitchen and spread or arranged between thick slices of bread. To cook them, put the sandwiches in an oiled basket-type hand grill, close, and brush the outsides of the sandwiches with oil or melted butter or margarine. Grill slowly over fire, turning, until nicely browned on both sides and heated within. Serve immediately.

Grilled Sandwich No. 1. Cheddar–Green Pepper–Garlic

Combine 1 cup shredded or grated Cheddar cheese, ¼ cup finely chopped green pepper, 2 tablespoons mayonnaise, and ½ garlic clove, finely minced. Proceed as above to make sandwiches with Herb Bread (see Index) or other bread.

Makes 4.

MENU SUGGESTION: A salad of sliced raw zucchini, mushrooms, and tomatoes with a little chopped scallion and your favorite salad dressing.

Grilled Sandwich No. 2. Muenster-Bacon-Scallion

Combine 1½ cups shredded Muenster cheese, 3 strips cooked and crumbled bacon, 1 large or 2 small scallions (including some of green part), finely chopped, and 2½ tablespoons mayonnaise. Proceed as above to make sandwiches with Black Peasant Bread (see Index) or bought dark bread.

Makes 4.

MENU SUGGESTION: Salad made with little red potatoes.

Grilled Sandwich No. 3. Blue Cheese–Turkey–Salami

Cream together 2 tablespoons softened butter or margarine and 2 tablespoons crumbled blue cheese. Spread on 8 slices Danish rye or pumpernickel, or similar bread. Arrange ½ pound sliced turkey breast meat on half of the bread slices, dividing equally. Arrange 3 ounces Danish salami (sliced paper-thin, casing removed) over the turkey, dividing equally. Put remaining bread slices over salami, buttered side down. Proceed as above to grill sandwiches.

Makes 4.

MENU SUGGESTION: Celery knob (celeriac) salad made of cooked and sliced or shredded celery knob marinated in refrigerator in lemon juice, oil, salt, and pepper.

Grilled Sandwich No. 4. Tangy Crab-Shrimp

Combine ½ pound picked-over and shredded lump crabmeat or canned crabmeat, ½ cup concentrated cream of shrimp soup (if not available, substitute other cream of seafood soup or cream of mushroom soup), 1 tablespoon lemon juice, ½ teaspoon dry mustard, ½ teaspoon salt, freshly ground pepper to taste, and a dash of Tabasco sauce. Proceed as above to make sandwiches with Four Grain Bread (see Index) or bought whole-grain bread.

Makes 4.

MENU SUGGESTION: Chinese cabbage salad with chopped sweet red pepper, a little scallion and parsley, and mayonnaise dressing.

Grilled Sandwich No. 5. Ham-Mushroom

Sauté 1 cup sliced mushrooms in 1 tablespoon butter or margarine until lightly browned. Combine with 1 cup chopped or ground ham, ¼ cup sour cream, ½ teaspoon Dijon mustard, and freshly ground pepper to taste. Proceed as above to make sandwiches with Cheddar Bread (see Index) or bought cheese bread.

Makes 4.

MENU SUGGESTION: Kidney bean salad with onion rings, chopped celery, and little cubes of Monterey Jack cheese. Use your favorite dressing.

CHORIZO DOGS

Have a chorizo dog once and you'll probably forget about hot dogs forever. Chorizos are Spanish sausages shaped more or less like hot dogs, only a little shorter and fatter, but there the similarity ends. Chorizos are gently spiced and flavored with paprika, which also gives them a pleasing bright color. They don't contain garlic, but have a flavor all their own. They can be found in nearly any Spanish grocery store; if you don't see them, ask for them, as they're not always out in view. If no place near you sells fresh ones, look for them in cans. Or get a friend who lives in a city where there are such stores to send you some chorizos in the mail. They'll survive a trip by parcel post in cool weather if they're sent by special handling, and you can stock up, since chorizos will keep for some time in the freezer.

chorizos
French bread or skinny Italian bread

Prick chorizos all over with a fork. Grill over fire about 5 minutes, turning. Cut bread into lengths a little longer than the chorizos, and slit open down one side without cutting all the way through. When chorizos are ready, pop them into the bread and gobble them up. Don't interfere with their distinct flavor by putting anything at all on them—save the ketchup and mustard for another day.

MENU SUGGESTION: Gazpacho.

SESAME VEALBURGERS

1 egg, beaten
1 tablespoon tomato paste
1 teaspoon salt
freshly ground pepper to taste
2 tablespoons sesame seed
¼ cup wheat germ
1 tablespoon grated onion
1 pound ground veal
1 loaf Italian bread
softened butter
Parmesan, Romano, or Sardo cheese

Combine egg, tomato paste, salt, pepper, sesame seed, wheat germ, and onion in a bowl. Add ground veal and mix until thoroughly blended. Divide into 4 equal parts and shape into patties. Cut bread in half lengthwise and butter cut sides liberally. Sprinkle butter generously with cheese and press down so that it sticks to the butter.

Arrange vealburgers in oiled basket-type hand grill and grill over fire, turning, until nicely browned on both sides. Meanwhile, toast bread over fire, cheese side down.

Put bread halves together and cut into 4 wedges. Slip a vealburger into each wedge. Serve immediately.

Makes 4 servings.

MENU SUGGESTION: Thick slices of onion, brushed with melted butter or margarine, and grilled over coals until crisply done and slightly glazed.

TURKISH SHISH KEBOB IN PITA BREAD

½ cup olive oil

¼ cup lemon juice

1 medium onion, chopped

2 bay leaves, torn into pieces

2 teaspoons marjoram

2 teaspoons salt

freshly ground pepper to taste

1½ pounds lean lamb cut into ¾-inch
   cubes

3 tomatoes, finely chopped

1 tablespoon fresh basil, chopped, or 1
   teaspoon dry basil

oil-and-vinegar dressing, or vinaigrette
   dressing (see Index)

6 pita breads (preferably whole wheat—
   bought or see Index)

Combine oil and lemon juice in bowl large enough to hold the lamb cubes. Put the chopped onion through a food processor or blender until pulverized and add to the oil–lemon juice mixture. Add bay leaves, marjoram, salt, and pepper, and combine. Add the lamb cubes and toss well. Cover and refrigerate for 6–24 hours, turning several times.

Drain and arrange on skewers and grill over fire 10–20 minutes, turning and brushing with the marinade, until nicely browned and cooked through.

Combine tomatoes and basil and add enough dressing to moisten. Toss well. Take lamb off skewers. Split pita breads open on side about ⅓ of the way around. Fill each with a spoonful of tomato, equal amount of lamb cubes, and another spoonful of tomatoes. Serve immediately.

Makes 6.

MENU SUGGESTION: Bennetta's Artichoke-Rice Salad (see Index) or your own version of this salad.

TRAILSIDE SANDWICHES

1 2½-ounce jar dried beef, shredded
½ cup chili sauce
1 large dill pickle, finely chopped
2 tablespoons mayonnaise
4 hamburger rolls (preferably whole wheat
    —see Index: Crusty Whole Wheat
    Hamburger Rolls)
softened butter or margarine
4 slices American cheese

Combine beef, chili sauce, pickle, and mayonnaise. Open rolls and toast insides over fire. Butter the toasted rolls. Spoon filling onto roll bottoms. Cover each with a slice of cheese. Put on tops of rolls. Wrap each sandwich in aluminum foil, tucking in ends well. Arrange on grill and heat slowly, turning, for about 20 minutes. Serve immediately.

Makes 4.

MENU SUGGESTION: Lettuce wedges with creamy dressing.

SPECTACULAR SALMON-DILL SLICES

4 salmon steaks cut about ¾ inch thick
kosher salt or other coarse salt
½ stick butter or margarine
2 tablespoons lemon juice
1 egg
½ cup sour cream
3 tablespoons chopped fresh dill, loosely
    packed, or 1 tablespoon dried dill weed
¼ teaspoon salt
freshly ground pepper to taste
1 loaf Italian bread with sesame seeds

Wash salmon steaks and dry with paper towels. Sprinkle lightly with salt.

Melt butter in a small saucepan. Add the lemon juice and combine.

Beat egg in a small bowl until thick and pale. Add sour cream, dill, salt, and pepper, and mix well. Set aside.

Arrange steaks in an oiled hand grill. Grill over fire a few minutes on each side, basting with the lemon-butter mixture. Take care not to overcook the salmon. While it is grilling, cut bread in half lengthwise and pull out some of soft inner part, reserving for another use. Toast cut sides of bread over fire. Brush toasted sides with lemon-butter mixture. Put bread on a long platter. Remove the bones from the salmon and arrange the salmon inside the bread. Spoon some of sour cream–dill mixture over the salmon, and serve the balance with the sandwiches so each person can add his own. Close the loaf of bread and cut in 2-inch slices. Serve immediately. Makes about 8 servings.

MENU SUGGESTION: Ginger-Lime Cucumber Pickles (see Index) or other cucumber pickles.

HOT DOGS WITH STREET VENDOR-STYLE ONIONS

3 tablespoons vegetable oil
4 cups onions cut in quarters and sliced
crosswise
1½ tablespoons sweet paprika
¼ teaspoon cumin
¾ teaspoon salt
freshly ground pepper to taste
8 hot dogs
8 hot dog rolls (preferably whole wheat)

Heat oil slightly in a heavy skillet and add onions, tossing until coated with oil. Add paprika, cumin, salt, and pepper, and toss again. Cover and simmer over low heat (or gentle coals) about 25 minutes, stirring often, without allowing onions to brown. Onions should be just a little firm when finished. If mixture becomes dry, add a few tablespoons water.

Meanwhile, grill the hot dogs. Open hot dog rolls and toast cut sides over fire. Put hot dogs in rolls and spoon the onion mixture over them, dividing equally. Serve immediately.

Makes 6.

MENU SUGGESTION: Carrot and celery sticks.

GUASTIEDDE SANDWICH

6 Italian sausages (sweet and/or hot)
6 hard rolls
1½ cups ricotta cheese
1 small package mozzarella cheese
vegetable oil, preferably olive oil

Grill sausages very slowly over fire, turning often, until lightly browned and well cooked through. Set on a plate and cut into ¼-inch slices, retaining any liquid that oozes out when slicing. Cut rolls in half horizontally and toast, cut side down, over fire. Arrange sausage slices in rolls, dividing equally.

Spoon ¼ cup ricotta over the sausage slices in each sandwich. Slice mozzarella ¼ inch thick and arrange a layer over the ricotta in each sandwich. Drizzle the sausage drippings on insides of tops of rolls; if there are no drippings, brush with oil. Wrap each sandwich in oiled aluminum foil, sealing ends well. Place over fire and heat slowly, turning, about 10 minutes until cheese has melted and sandwich is hot. Serve immediately.

Makes 6.

MENU SUGGESTION: Italian Salad (see Index).

RACY RACLETTE BURGERS

1 pound ground beef
2 tablespoons Sauce Diable (such as
    Colman's brand)
¼ teaspoon salt
freshly ground pepper to taste
4 slices raclette cheese about 4 inches
    square (this is a cheese from Switzer-
    land)
1 long loaf sourdough French bread or 4
    sourdough rolls
gherkins, pickled baby corn, and/or
    pickled onions

Combine ground beef, Sauce Diable, salt, and pepper, and shape into 4 patties. Grill over fire on one side. Turn and put a slice of cheese on each. Slice bread or rolls horizontally and toast cut sides over fire. (If you have a kettle-type cooker, put the cover on at this point so the cheese melts faster. The bread will toast at the same time.)

When cheese has melted, put hamburgers inside rolls, or cut the bread into 4 equal parts and put a hamburger in each wedge. Tuck some of the pickles inside each sandwich, cutting in half lengthwise if necessary to flatten them a little. (If you prefer you can serve the pickles on the plate with each sandwich rather than putting them inside the sandwiches.) Close sandwiches and serve immediately.

Makes 4.

MENU SUGGESTION: French-fried onion rings.

HAWAIIAN SCALLOP SANDWICH

1 cup pineapple juice

1/3 cup soy sauce (preferably ketjap manis,
     which is an Indonesian soy sauce, or
     tamari soy sauce. If using tamari soy
     sauce or ordinary soy sauce, add 3
     tablespoons honey.)

1 tablespoon butter or margarine

1 tablespoon chopped fresh ginger root or
     canned green ginger root

freshly ground pepper to taste

1½ tablespoons cornstarch

20 large scallops

4 hot dog rolls (whole wheat or white) or
     French bread cut in 6-inch lengths

Combine ¾ cup of the pineapple juice, soy sauce
(and honey, if required), butter, ginger root, and pepper
in a small saucepan. Bring to boil, stirring until butter
has melted. Combine cornstarch with remaining juice
and stir into sauce, cooking until thickened. Remove
from stove and cool to lukewarm.

Meanwhile, wash scallops and pat dry with paper
towels. Combine scallops with pineapple–soy sauce
mixture in a bowl. Cover and refrigerate several hours,
turning once or twice during that time.

Arrange 5 scallops each on 4 flat skewers. Put the
pineapple–soy sauce mixture in a small saucepan,
cover, and set over fire to heat. Grill the scallops over
coals, turning, until just done. They take only a few
minutes on each side, so take care not to overcook and
toughen them.

Meanwhile, slit rolls or bread in half and remove some of the soft inside, reserving for another use. Toast cut sides of rolls or bread over fire. Set a skewer of cooked scallops in each roll and slide out the skewers. Spoon some of the hot pineapple–soy sauce mixture over the scallops. Pass remaining sauce for those who may want more.

Makes 4 servings.

MENU SUGGESTION: If you get your fire going early enough, bake some sweet potatoes, and later on some unpeeled bananas. These go nicely with the pineapple flavoring of the scallop sandwiches.

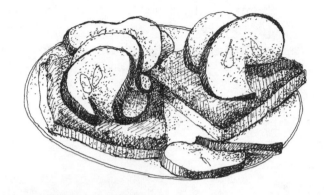

8. SANDWICHES FOR SNACK TIME

A morsel for a monarch.
—SHAKESPEARE, *Antony and Cleopatra*

We're a nation of snackers, no doubt about it, but there's no need to settle for the fast-food variety of snack when you can have an enticing sandwich. This chapter has toothsome sandwiches which you can enjoy after a ball game or card game, at an after-theater gathering, or as a midnight snack—in fact, any time when a snack is appropriate. The Danish sandwiches, for instance, are perfect for late-party snacks, the Potato Chip Crunch Sandwich will delight anyone of any age at any time, and the Mini Provençal Pissaladière provides a pleasing and less-filling treat than its sister the pizza after a brisk autumn walk or winter skiing.

Some of these snack sandwiches are substantial enough to serve as lunch-time sandwiches, and others can be worked into a lunch menu with the addition of a filling soup. Accompaniment and garnishing suggestions follow each recipe.

PIPERADE PITA

2 onions, thinly sliced

3 green peppers, quartered lengthwise and
   thinly sliced crosswise

½ garlic clove, minced

1 tablespoon butter or margarine

1 tablespoon vegetable oil

3 medium-size tomatoes, peeled, seeded,
   and chopped

½ teaspoon salt

freshly ground pepper to taste

1 teaspoon marjoram

6 eggs, beaten

4–6 pita breads, whole wheat or white
   (bought or see Index)

Sauté onions and green peppers with garlic in butter and oil until soft but not browned. Add tomatoes, salt, pepper, and marjoram, and cook over moderate heat about 5 minutes, stirring, until mixture is almost dry. Add eggs and cook, stirring gently with a wooden spoon, until eggs are set. Remove from stove.

Split pita breads open at edge about ⅓ of the way around. Fill with piperade mixture, dividing equally. Serve immediately.

Makes 4–6, depending on size of pita breads.

MENU SUGGESTION: Serve with pickled onions and black olives. (Little niçoise olives are nice if you can find them.)

WAFFLED SOHO SANDWICH

12 thin slices firm white bread ¼ inch
   thick (such as Pepperidge Farm Very
   Thin Sliced White Bread)
softened butter or margarine
½ cup freshly grated Parmesan, Romano,
   or Sardo cheese
2 tablespoons sweet vermouth

Select slices of bread that do not have any holes in
them. Trim crusts off evenly and butter one side of
each slice. Combine cheese and vermouth, tossing until
mixture just holds together. Spoon a heaping tablespoon of cheese mixture onto the unbuttered sides of
half the bread slices and spread out evenly without allowing cheese to go to edges. Top with remaining
bread, buttered sides out.

Meanwhile, preheat waffle iron on low setting.
Place sandwiches 2 at a time (or as many as waffle iron
will hold) in waffle iron and close tightly. If waffle iron
does not close all the way, press down on top until it
does. Bake about 2 minutes. Remove, and continue
until all sandwiches have been baked. They will be
very crisp, with a waffle pattern. Serve immediately.
   Makes 6.

MENU SUGGESTION: Marinated Avocado-Mushroom Mélange
(see Index).

NUTTED TUNA AND SPINACH SANDWICH

softened butter or margarine
8 slices Tomato Bread (see Index) or any
    preferred bread
1 6½-ounce can chunk or flake tuna
½ cup chopped walnuts
¼ teaspoon basil
⅓ cup mayonnaise
¼ teaspoon salt
freshly ground pepper to taste
spinach leaves, washed and thoroughly
    dried

Butter the bread slices. Combine tuna, walnuts, basil, mayonnaise, salt, and pepper, and spoon on half the slices, dividing equally. Spread out the tuna mixture evenly and cover with spinach leaves and remaining bread. Cut in half.

Makes 4.

MENU SUGGESTION: Make bacon olives by cutting bacon slices in half and wrapping around stuffed green olives. Anchor with toothpicks and broil, turning until bacon is crisp.

MINI PROVENÇAL PISSALADIÈRE

5 cups thinly sliced onions
4–6 tablespoons vegetable oil
½ teaspoon salt
freshly ground pepper to taste
1 16-ounce package fresh or frozen pizza
    dough, thawed
white flour
⅛ teaspoon oregano
6 flat anchovies
8 black olives (preferably Greek or Italian),
    each cut into 3 strips, pits removed
2 generous tablespoons grated Swiss cheese
2 generous tablespoons grated Parmesan
    cheese

Cook onions in 4 tablespoons oil in a skillet over low heat, adding salt and pepper. Turn and stir often until the onions are soft and translucent, about 25 minutes. Try to prevent any browning. Add a little more oil and lower the flame to very low if necessary. Remove from stove and allow to cool slightly while proceeding to shape dough.

Remove pizza dough from package and sprinkle with flour. Cut evenly into quarters. Shape each piece into a ball and flatten into a disk about 6 inches in diameter by patting with the hands on a floured board, or by holding the dough and pulling and shaping it into a circle. Arrange on greased baking sheets.

Preheat oven at 400°. Spoon onions equally over the disks and spread out evenly. Sprinkle with oregano. Cut anchovies in half crosswise and arrange 3 on each disk in wheel-spoke fashion. Arrange 2 strips of olive between each two spokes. Sprinkle cheese evenly over tops. Drizzle a small amount of vegetable oil over the cheese. Bake 25 minutes or until nicely browned and puffed. Serve immediately.

Makes 4.

MENU SUGGESTION: Sangria.

POTATO CHIP CRUNCH SANDWICH

4 strips bacon
softened butter or margarine
8 slices wheat germ bread (bought or see Index) or similar bread
peanut butter (preferably 100-percent-peanuts type)
1 bag potato chips

Sauté bacon until nicely browned. Drain on paper towel and cut in half crosswise. Butter 4 slices of bread. Spread peanut butter on remaining bread. Arrange a triple layer of potato chips (you can use broken ones if you wish) over the peanut butter. Arrange 2 pieces of bacon over the potato chips. Cover with buttered bread and cut sandwiches in half.

Makes 4.

MENU SUGGESTION: Radishes and cracked green olives as a garnish.

TOWERING EGGPLANT SANDWICH

These are striking, delicious, and inexpensive. If you have one left over and you're an eggplant lover, you'll enjoy it even more reheated in the oven the next day. If you aren't an eggplant lover, nothing will change your mind.

2 eggs
¼ cup milk
wheat germ
1 large or 2 medium eggplants, cut into 16
    slices ½ inch thick
vegetable oil
butter or margarine
12 slices tomato (3–5 tomatoes) ½ inch
    thick
4 thick slices Dill Bread (see Index) or any
    preferred bread of large size
tahini (ground sesame seed)
1 cup shredded Monterey Jack, Italian
    Fontina, or similar fast-melting cheese

Beat eggs lightly in a shallow soup plate. Add milk and stir. Pour wheat germ into another shallow soup plate. Dip eggplant slices, one at a time, in wheat germ, then beaten egg, and again in wheat germ. Sauté, a few at a time, in a tablespoon of oil and a tablespoon of butter until nicely browned on both sides, adding more oil and butter as needed. Set aside.

Sauté tomato slices lightly in same pan, adding oil and butter as needed, until nicely browned on both sides. Set aside.

Preheat broiler. Toast bread, butter it, and spread thinly with tahini. Stack eggplant and tomato slices alternately on toast, graduating from largest slices of eggplant on bottom to smallest on top. Sprinkle cheese equally over all. Place under broiler until nicely browned. Serve immediately.

Makes 4.

MENU SUGGESTION: Garnish with oil-cured black olives beside each towering sandwich. (Make sure the olives haven't been sprinkled with red pepper flakes unless you like them that way.)

CHAPPATI WITH TOMATO, CHEESE, AND SPROUTS

chappati (see Index—allow one for each
   sandwich)
miso (soy bean paste) or soy sauce
   (preferably tamari soy sauce)
sliced tomatoes
shredded cheese (any kind you like)
bean sprouts (fresh or canned and drained)

Make chappati and fold over while still hot. Spread inside of chappati lightly with miso and fill with a layer each of tomato slices, cheese, and bean sprouts, or omit miso and sprinkle filling with soy sauce to taste.

MENU SUGGESTION: Hot or iced herb tea, such as Red Zinger, or minted regular tea.

OYSTER BOX

6 rectangular hard rolls
softened butter or margarine
2 dozen oysters, removed from shells
celery salt
flour
1 egg
½ teaspoon Worcestershire sauce
cracker crumbs made by crushing buttery-
    type salted crackers (such as Ritz or Tuc
    crackers) with rolling pin
oil for frying
lemon juice
cocktail sauce (optional)

Cut tops off rolls. Pull out as much of soft part of rolls as possible, reserving for another use. Butter inside of rolls and put tops back on. Set aside.

Rinse oysters under cold running water to make certain any remaining bits of shell are washed off. Pat dry with paper towel. Sprinkle generously with celery salt.

Put some flour in a shallow soup plate. Beat the egg in another shallow soup plate and add the Worcestershire sauce. Put the cracker crumbs in another shallow soup plate. Heat the oil to about 375° in a wok or deep fryer. Do not allow it to become hot enough to smoke.

Dip the oysters, one at a time, in the flour, then the beaten egg, then the crumbs, and put in a skimmer or wire basket. Fry a few at a time for about 30 seconds until golden. Do not overcook or the oysters will toughen. Drain on paper towels.

When all oysters have been fried, arrange 4 oysters in each roll. Squeeze lemon juice over the oysters. Put tops on rolls and serve with cocktail sauce if desired. Makes 6.

MENU SUGGESTION: Cucumber sticks or Crunchy Danish Cucumber Salad (see Index).

DANSK SMØRREBRØD: FIVE BEAUTIFUL DANISH OPEN-FACED SANDWICHES

Here are the general directions for making the following sandwiches or any Danish open-faced sandwich (and are any sandwiches more beautiful?). Cream butter until soft and butter all bread thickly. Use dark or light rye, pumpernickel, any Danish bread of wheat and/or rye, and occasionally firm white bread. The ingredients used to top the bread should be applied lavishly. Take time to arrange the ingredients and garnish the sandwiches nicely. While they should not look fussy, they should look attractive, almost like little works of art. Do them any way you like, or follow the instructions below for some typical arrangements. These sandwiches are eaten with knife and fork. You can't pick them up because there's too much piled on top. Allow 2 sandwiches for each person.

Most of the ingredients are easily obtainable in any food store, but a few, such as herring tidbits imported from Sweden and Danish smoked eel, may require some scouting to locate. Besides the sandwiches below, other possibilities are roast beef with horseradish, ham (Danish if possible), roast pork with red cabbage, Danish meatballs split open, fillet of plaice or sole with tartar sauce and lemon, Swiss cheese with radish slices, sardines, rolled veal, tongue, and so on. Garnishes include scrambled eggs, tomatoes, pickles, fried mushrooms, currant jelly, lingonberries (in cans or jars from Sweden), pickles, chives, and so forth.

Danish Sandwich No. 1. Shrimp: Butter firm white bread. Place a small leaf of Boston or similar buttery-type lettuce on bread, but do not allow it to overlap the bread to any extent; shape it to fit. Depending on the size of cooked chilled shrimp you use, make 2, 4, or 6 rows of overlapping shrimps over the lettuce. With pastry bag fitted with a star tip, pipe a thick band of mayonnaise down the very center between the rows of shrimp. Decorate with a very thin slice of lemon which has been slashed to the center in one place, with one side twisted up and the other side twisted down and around and spread out.

Danish Sandwich No. 2. Liver Pâté: Trim Danish dark rye bread to square shape and butter it. Cover with a slice of liver pâté the same size, or spread the pâté on evenly and smoothly, just as thick at edges as in the center. Cut two very thin slices of unpeeled, unwaxed cucumber. Slash each to center in one place and shape as above for lemon slice. Lay cucumber twists on top of the pâté. Cut two small squares from a thin slice of pickled beet and nestle one in each cucumber twist.

Danish Sandwich No. 3. Smoked Eel and Danish Cheese: Cut Danish pumpernickel bread in rectangular shape and butter it. On half of the bread place a slice of Danish smoked eel cut to fit. On the other half place a slice of Danish cheese, such as Havarti or Danbo, or other cheese such as Muenster, cut to fit. Sprinkle with chopped chives.

Danish Sandwich No. 4. Danish Salami with Jellied Consommé: Butter Danish rye or other oval bread. Fold 3 slices of Danish salami in half. Arrange on bread in fan shape. Cut a half circle of jellied consommé and place at the base of fan. Garnish with small parsley sprig.

Danish Sandwich No. 5. Herring Tidbits or Anchovies and Hard-cooked Egg Slices: Butter Danish pumpernickel bread. Arrange center slices of hard-cooked egg on bread. Lay herring tidbits or flat anchovies over egg slices. Decorate with fresh dill sprig.

MENU SUGGESTION: Pickled beets, potato salad, or Crunchy Danish Cucumber Salad (see Index).

BÉARNAISE OMELET STUFFED
BRIOCHE WEDGES

1 large brioche, about 6 inches in diameter
    at widest part (see Index or use bought
    brioche)
¼ cup (approximately) melted butter
¾ cup sliced mushrooms
4 freshly cooked or canned asparagus
    spears, cut in ½-inch slices
2 artichoke bottoms, cut in half and thinly
    sliced
3 eggs
3 tablespoons Béarnaise sauce (such as
    Butternut Farm brand, or homemade)

Preheat oven at 200°. With sharp-pointed knife
carve down and around to remove topknot from
brioche. Using a sharp knife for cutting and a spoon for
scooping, remove as much of the inside of the brioche
as possible, leaving about a half-inch shell. (Reserve
scooped-out crumbs for another use.) Brush inside of
brioche with melted butter. Set on baking sheet or in
baking pan and warm in oven while preparing stuffing.
    Sauté mushrooms in 1 tablespoon melted butter in
a medium-size skillet until lightly browned. Add
asparagus and artichoke bottoms and toss lightly. Remove from heat and set aside. Beat eggs lightly with
wire whisk. Add mushroom mixture to eggs and stir
lightly. Add 2 tablespoons melted butter to skillet and
set over brisk flame. Add egg mixture and scramble it.
Spoon into brioche. Spoon Béarnaise sauce evenly over
eggs. Set topknot back on brioche and set brioche on
serving plate.

Serve immediately, cutting into quarters, pie-fashion, at the table.

Makes 4 servings.

MENU SUGGESTION: Freshly brewed coffee is all that's needed with this beautiful sandwich.

GRILLED BLUE CHEESE AND ASPARAGUS SANDWICH

**Dark Soy-Carob Bread (see Index) or
    bought dark bread
mayonnaise
tomato slices
asparagus tips (freshly cooked or canned)
lemon juice
Norwegian or Danish blue or Gorgonzola
    cheese, thinly sliced (most easily done
    with wire-blade cheese cutter)**

Preheat broiler. Lay out 1 slice bread for each sandwich. Spread with mayonnaise. Cover completely with tomato slices, filling in small spaces with pieces cut from tomato slices. Arrange 2 or 3 asparagus tips on each sandwich. Sprinkle with a little lemon juice. Cover with cheese. Arrange on baking sheet and broil until cheese is bubbly and lightly browned. Serve immediately.

MENU SUGGESTION: Mustard pickles or Pickled Carrot Slims (see Index).

MOZZARELLA EN CARROZZA

8 slices thinly sliced firm white bread ¼
   inch thick (such as Pepperidge Farm Very
   Thin Sliced White Bread)
1 8-ounce package whole-milk mozzarella
   cheese
2 eggs
2 tablespoons milk
generous pinch salt
freshly ground pepper to taste
wheat germ or fine dry breadcrumbs
olive oil or other vegetable oil
watercress or olives (optional garnish)

Select bread slices that do not have any holes in
them. Stack up 4 slices at a time and trim crusts evenly.
Keep bread slices in sets of 2 so edges of sandwiches
will be even. Cut 4 slices mozzarella from broad side
of the cheese. Set 1 each on 4 bread slices. The cheese
should be about ¼ inch narrower than the bread all
around. Place remaining slices of bread on top of
cheese. With fingers press edges together all around.

Beat eggs lightly in a shallow soup plate. Stir in
milk, salt, and pepper. Put some wheat germ or breadcrumbs in another shallow soup plate. Heat oil in a
heavy skillet until quite hot, but do not allow to become near the smoking point.

Dip sandwiches, one at a time, in egg mixture,
turning to coat both sides and making sure each of the
edges is coated. Dip the edges only in wheat germ or
breadcrumbs to seal in the cheese. Fry 2 sandwiches at
a time in the hot oil, turning to brown both sides nicely.
Drain on paper towels. Garnish with watercress or

olives placed beside each sandwich if desired. Serve immediately.

Makes 4.

MENU SUGGESTION: Prosciutto and melon.

Variation: Arrange 1 or 2 flat anchovies over the mozzarella in each sandwich before sealing the edges.

LASHING TONGUE SANDWICH

½ stick butter or margarine
3–4 teaspoons horseradish
8 slices Tomato Bread (see Index) or any
    preferred bread
½ pound sliced cooked tongue
Boston lettuce or other buttery-type lettuce

Cream the butter and add horseradish. Spread on bread slices. Arrange tongue on half of bread slices. Cover with lettuce and remaining bread. Cut in half or quarters.

Makes 4.

MENU SUGGESTION: French-fried Mushrooms (see Index) or French-fried potatoes.

CRABMEAT-AVOCADO SANDWICH

¼ cup sour cream
2 tablespoons lemon juice
1 teaspoon dill weed or 1 tablespoon
   chopped fresh dill
¼ teaspoon dry mustard
½ teaspoon salt
freshly ground pepper to taste
½ pound fresh lump crabmeat or canned
   crabmeat, picked over
4 slices rye bread
softened butter or margarine
1 ripe avocado

Combine sour cream, lemon juice, dill, mustard, salt, and pepper. Add crabmeat and toss. Cover and chill.

Toast bread and butter it. Arrange on serving plates. Spoon crabmeat mixture over each and spread out evenly. Peel and slice avocado thinly. Arrange slices over crabmeat, dividing equally. Serve immediately.

Makes 4.

MENU SUGGESTION: Cups of cold cucumber soup.

FRENCH BAGUETTE WITH PÂTÉ AND CORNICHONS

**fresh pâté (country pâté if available),
canned Strasbourg pâté (imported from
France), or, failing that, an inexpensive
canned pâté which you can perk up with
brandy and some green peppercorns
French baguette, or any French or Italian
bread, as skinny as you can find
cornichons (little French sour gherkins) or
other very small sour pickles**

Put a slice of pâté, a few slices of French bread, and a few pickles on each person's plate, arranging in an attractive way. Supply each person with a small spreader for transporting the pâté to the bread.

MENU SUGGESTION: A white wine such as an Alsatian Riesling would be nice with this. If you wanted to make this a sturdier snack you could preface it with cups of canned cream of potato soup thinned with milk and whirled in a blender or food processor with 2½ ounces Boursin Cheese with Garlic and Herbs before heating.

GREEK SALAD SANDWICH

1 14-ounce can artichoke hearts in brine,
   drained
1 large rib celery, split in half lengthwise
   and finely sliced
1 large tomato, peeled and thinly sliced
3 or 4 thin slices red onion, broken into
   rings
6 canned stuffed baby eggplants, sliced
   crosswise (optional)
4 teaspoons chopped anchovies
2 tablespoons lemon juice
2 tablespoons vegetable oil
1 teaspoon salt
freshly ground pepper to taste
softened butter or margarine
12 slices Black Peasant Bread (see Index)
   or bought dark bread
¼ pound feta cheese
12–18 Calamata olives or other black olives
   (preferably Greek), pits removed, sliced
romaine or Boston lettuce

If artichokes are small (20–25 per can), cut in half. If they are larger, cut in quarters. Put in bowl with celery, tomato, onion, eggplants, and anchovies. Shake lemon juice, oil, salt, and pepper together in a jar and pour over the artichoke mixture. Toss gently. Cover and refrigerate several hours, tossing once or twice during that time.

Drain artichoke mixture. Butter the bread slices. Spoon artichoke mixture on half the bread slices, dividing equally. Cut cheese into slices and arrange over artichoke mixture. Arrange olive slices over the cheese, dividing equally. Top with lettuce and close sandwiches with remaining slices of buttered bread. Cut in half. Serve immediately.

Makes 6.

MENU SUGGESTION: Serve Greek olives and Greek Salonika peppers as a garnish alongside the sandwiches. Red wine goes well with these sandwiches.

9. SANDWICHES FOR COCKTAIL TIME

The gay, the gay and festive scene.
—CHARLES DICKENS, *Our Mutual Friend*

Dutch, French, Scottish, Greek, Iranian, Indian, Chinese, Mexican, and English-inspired cocktail sandwiches are only a few of the choices you have among the tempting morsels here, each designed to bring new life to the cocktail sandwich tray. Mix them, match them, or serve just one kind. Serve them along with other hors d'oeuvres if you like. There are both hot and cold sandwiches, some open-faced and others closed—something to please everyone.

DUTCH DEVILS

1¾ cups grated Dutch Leyden cheese (or
    Noekkelost or Danbo cheese)
¼ cup mayonnaise
1 tablespoon grated onion
¼ cup deviled ham
2 teaspoons Dijon mustard
1 teaspoon horseradish
freshly ground pepper to taste
cocktail pumpernickel rounds or squares

Combine ingredients, except pumpernickel, in
order listed. Spread on pumpernickel, or pack the mixture into a small crock or ramekin and serve with the
pumpernickel.

Makes about 3 dozen.

MUSHROOM SAUSAGE ROUNDS

18 mushrooms about 1¼ inches in
    diameter
¼ pound sausage meat
18 rye-toast rounds about 1½ inches in
    diameter (bought or cut from rye
    bread with cookie cutter and
    toasted)
18 thin slices mozzarella cheese

Remove stems from mushrooms and reserve for
another use. Wash and dry mushroom caps, or wipe
them clean. Sauté sausage meat until it has lost all its
red color, breaking up with a fork as it cooks.

Preheat oven at 350°. Put a spoonful of sausage
meat on each toast round. Place a mushroom cap,
round side up, to cover sausage meat. Arrange on baking sheet. Place a piece of mozzarella on each mushroom. It should be large enough to cover the mushroom
cap completely but not large enough to touch the baking sheet.* Bake 10 minutes, until cheese has melted.
If not browned, run under broiler a minute or two.
Serve immediately.

Makes 18.

* This can be made ahead, covered, and refrigerated at this point.

SAVORY SARDINE SANDWICHES

1 5½-ounce can sardines in tomato sauce
1 slice cooked crumbled bacon or 1 table-
    spoon bacon bits
1 tablespoon mayonnaise
2 tablespoons finely chopped celery
1 tablespoon lemon juice
1 teaspoon grated onion
freshly ground pepper to taste
15–18 slices soft white bread
softened butter or margarine
1 egg yolk
2 tablespoons milk

Preheat oven at 400°. Mash sardines with sauce, using a fork, and add bacon, mayonnaise, celery, lemon juice, onion, and pepper.

Trim crusts from bread. With rolling pin, flatten each slice. Cut in half and butter each piece. Spoon about 1 teaspoon sardine filling in center of each, keeping filling away from edges. Fold over to enclose filling and press edges together with fingers, then with tines of a fork. Arrange on baking sheet. Beat egg yolk lightly, stir in milk, and brush over each square. Bake 10 minutes or until lightly browned. Serve immediately.

Makes 2½–3 dozen.

TARAMOSALATA TOASTS

This is a traditional Greek appetizer, fluffy and beautifully peachy-pink. It makes a fantastic cocktail sandwich. Although you can buy good taramosalata already made in a jar, the seasoning and texture will be finer if you make it yourself from tarama caviar, which is carp roe. Both the tarama caviar and taramosalata are available in glass jars in specialty food stores, delicatessens, and Greek and Middle Eastern food stores. Both products must be kept refrigerated.

> **5 ounces (generous ½ cup) tarama caviar**
>   **(such as Krinos brand)**
> **2 slices white bread, crusts removed**
> **water**
> **2 tablespoons lemon juice**
> **1 tablespoon grated onion**
> **½ cup olive oil**
> **thinly sliced firm dark or light bread**

Place caviar in food processor or blender and blend until pale and creamy, stopping once or twice to scrape down sides if necessary. Soak the bread in water for five minutes, squeeze out excess water, and add the bread to the cavair, along with lemon juice and onion. Blend again until thoroughly combined, scraping down sides if necessary. Turn on machine and add oil in a fine stream until it has all been absorbed and mixture is very fluffy. Transfer to a bowl or glass jar. Cover tightly and refrigerate until well chilled. To serve, toast bread, trim crusts off, and cut each slice into quarters. Spread with taramosalata. Makes 2 cups.

SUGGESTED GARNISH: Slivers of Greek black olives or pimiento squares or strips.

SCOTCH SALMON ELÉGANT

If you just got elected mayor, won a beauty contest, or passed through customs without having your bags inspected, you owe it to yourself to celebrate. Smash your piggybank and head for the market to buy a few slices of Scotch salmon. Serve it this way and you won't be sorry.

pumpernickel bread (preferably Lithuanian pumpernickel), thinly sliced
1 package Boursault cheese (if not available, substitute Boursin Natural cheese. Do not use Boursin with Garlic and Herbs), at room temperature. One package Boursault will make about 18 sandwiches.
thinly sliced Scotch salmon
capers

Cut rounds of pumpernickel with a small cookie cutter. Cream the cheese until very soft and spread about ¼ inch thick on bread rounds. Cut rounds of Scotch salmon close together, using the same cutter you used for the bread. (Eat all the salmon scraps yourself.) Set salmon on top of cheese. Put a tiny dab of cheese in the center of each salmon round and top with a few capers as a garnish.

GREEN CHILI HOTS

1 loaf French or Italian bread
1 4-ounce can jalapeño or other green
    chilies
1 stick butter or margarine
1 small garlic clove, minced
¼ cup finely chopped pitted green olives
½ cup mayonnaise
1½ cups grated Cheddar or similar cheese

Preheat broiler with shelf about 7 inches from heat. Slice bread ½–¾ inch thick and toast on one side. Remove as many seeds from the chilies as you wish— the more seeds, the hotter the sandwiches. If you re- move all the seeds they won't be hot at all. Chop the chilies finely. Soften butter and blend with the chilies. Add garlic and olives. Spread on untoasted side of bread. Blend mayonnaise and cheese and spread over the chili mixture. Arrange on baking sheet and broil until bubbly and lightly browned. Serve immediately.

Makes about 2 dozen.

GRILLED CHUTNEY CHEESE SANDWICH

**thinly sliced Swedish lympa bread (bought
   or see Index), firm white bread cut ¼
   inch thick, or firm-textured French sourdough bread cut ¼ inch thick
Cheddar cheese
softened butter or margarine
hot mango chutney or Major Grey's
   chutney
curry powder**

Cut bread in rounds or squares with cookie cutter
or knife. Cut cheese in same size rounds or squares.
Butter bread. Place slice of cheese on unbuttered side of
half the bread. Spread chutney on unbuttered side of
remaining bread. Sprinkle curry powder over the
cheese. Put sandwiches together, buttered sides out.
Sauté in skillet, turning, until golden on both sides and
cheese is melted. Serve immediately.

CHINESE SHRIMP TOAST

6 slices square white bread
½ pound shelled and deveined raw shrimp
¼ pound ground pork
2 tablespoons minced onion
1 teaspoon sugar
1 teaspoon salt
¼ teaspoon sesame oil or vegetable oil
1 tablespoon cornstarch
1 egg, beaten
fine dry breadcrumbs
vegetable oil for frying

Trim crusts from bread slices and lay out slices to dry slightly, about 15 minutes. Meanwhile, chop shrimp coarsely and combine with pork, onion, sugar, salt, oil, and cornstarch. Add beaten egg. Spread evenly over the bread slices. Cut each slice into 4 triangles. Sprinkle generously with breadcrumbs and pat lightly so crumbs will adhere.

Heat oil in wok or deep fryer to 375°. Fry the toast a few pieces at a time, shrimp side down, until brown at edges. Turn and brown other side. Drain on paper towels. Serve immediately.

Makes 24.

SUGGESTED GARNISH: Chopped parsley.

WALNUTWICHES

⅓ small garlic clove, cut up (too much
     garlic will overpower the other ingredients)
1 cup shelled walnuts
1 tablespoon vegetable oil
cayenne pepper to taste
½ teaspoon tarragon
generous pinch of thyme
¼ teaspoon salt
Oatmeal Bread (see Index) or similar bread,
     toasted and cut into small squares or rounds

Put garlic in food processor or blender and blend until puréed. Add walnuts and oil and blend until puréed, stopping when necessary to scrape down sides with rubber spatula. Add cayenne pepper, tarragon, thyme, and salt, and blend again. Spread on toast pieces or pack into a crock and serve with toast pieces.

Makes about 2 dozen.

BOURSIN OMELET BITES

1 2¾-ounce package Boursin Cheese with
   Garlic and Herbs
2 tablespoons milk or cream
1 loaf Italian bread
softened butter or margarine
6 eggs
2 tablespoons water
pinch of salt
dash of Tabasco sauce
freshly ground pepper

Soften cheese in a bowl. Add milk or cream a tablespoon at a time, beating until well blended. Set aside. Cut 15 center slices from the bread, each ½ inch thick, and butter both sides. Sauté in skillet, turning, until nicely browned on both sides. Arrange on a hot plate.

Beat eggs lightly. Combine water, salt, and Tabasco sauce in a cup and add to the eggs, mixing well. Put a teaspoon of butter in a small skillet, crêpe pan, or omelet pan measuring about 6 inches across the bottom, and heat until bubbly, tilting pan. Add 2 tablespoons of the egg mixture all at once, tilting pan to coat evenly, and cook until just set. Remove from heat.

Place a small spoonful of cheese mixture in the center of omelet. Run spatula around edges of omelet. Fold two opposite sides of omelet over cheese mixture to overlap at center. Fold ends over to overlap at center, forming a square or rectangle. Set omelet on a piece of sautéed bread. Cover with aluminum foil.

Continue making omelets until egg mixture has been used up. Sprinkle omelets lightly with freshly ground pepper. Serve immediately (but they will still taste very good if they cool to room temperature).

Makes about 15.

SWEET RED ITALIAN ONION SANDWICHES

1 sweet red Italian onion*
firm white bread sliced ¼ inch thick (such as Pepperidge Farm Very Thin Sliced White Bread)
mayonnaise
freshly ground pepper
finely chopped parsley

Slice onion in tissue-paper-thin slices. With a round cookie cutter 1½ inches or more in diameter cut twice as many bread circles as you want sandwiches. Spread mayonnaise on all. Top half the circles with 1 same-size onion slice. Sprinkle a few grains of pepper on the onion. Put remaining bread circles over the onion, mayonnaise side down. Spread sandwich edges with mayonnaise. Roll the mayonnaised rims in parsley.

* One onion will make dozens of sandwiches. Bermuda onion may be substituted for sweet red Italian onion if desired.

SEVICHE IN TOAST CUPS

1/2 pound shelled deveined shrimp
1/2 pound uncooked white-meat fish (flounder,
    halibut, etc.), all bones removed
5 very thin slices lemon, each cut into eighths
2 scallions, including some of green part,
    thinly sliced
1/4 cup pitted black olives, sliced or coarsely
    cut up
1 tablespoon chopped pimiento
1/4 cup lemon juice
2 tablespoons vegetable oil
1/2 tablespoon wine vinegar
1/2 garlic clove, finely minced
1/4 bay leaf, crumbled
1/2 teaspoon dry mustard
1/8 teaspoon cayenne pepper
1/2 teaspoon salt
freshly ground black pepper to taste
thinly sliced white bread

Poach shrimp in simmering water for 1 minute. Remove from water, rinse under cold running water, drain, and chop coarsely. Cut fish into small chunks and combine with the shrimp in a bowl. Add lemon pieces, scallions, olives, and pimiento, and toss gently. In another bowl combine lemon juice, oil, vinegar, garlic, bay leaf, mustard, cayenne pepper, salt, and black pepper, and pour over fish mixture. Cover and refrigerate 2–4 hours, tossing gently once or twice during that time.

Meanwhile, preheat oven at 400°. With round cookie cutter about 2¾ inches in diameter, cut circles from slices of bread. Gently shape and mold each into one of the depressions of tiny cupcake or muffin tins to form bread cups. Set in oven for 2–4 minutes until lightly browned, watching carefully to see that they do not become too dark. Remove from oven and cool in tins.

To serve, drain fish mixture very well, spoon into toast cups, and serve immediately.

Makes 3–4 dozen.

SUGGESTED GARNISH: Small strips or squares of avocado.

MINI CROQUE MONSIEURS

Prepare Croque Monsieur (see Index). Cut each sandwich into 9 squares with a sharp knife. Arrange on tray or serving plate and serve immediately.

Two regular-size Croque Monsieurs will make enough Mini Croque Monsieurs for 6 persons.

RICOTTA CAPONATA CANAPE

1 cup ricotta cheese

1 3¾-ounce can caponata (an eggplant
    appetizer—made by Progresso and others)
    or equivalent amount homemade caponata
    (see Index)

½ teaspoon horseradish

2 tablespoons lemon juice

½ garlic clove, finely minced

1 teaspoon Dijon mustard

¼ teaspoon salt

cayenne pepper to taste

freshly ground pepper to taste

whole wheat Italian bread (bought or see
    Index) or white Italian bread

softened butter or margarine

Combine all ingredients, except bread and butter, in order listed. Put through food processor or blender just long enough to break up the eggplant allowing it to become puréed. Turn into a small bowl. Cover and chill.

Cut slices of Italian bread ½ inch thick. Toast and butter them and cut in half crosswise. Spread chilled ricotta-caponata mixture on toast pieces.

Makes 2 dozen or more.

MONGOLIAN STEAK TARTAR SANDWICHES

softened butter or margarine
Dijon mustard to taste
firm dark rye or pumpernickel cocktail squares
    or rounds
1 pound round steak (or other good flavorful
    lean beef), ground
1 teaspoon Worcestershire sauce
dash of Tabasco sauce
grated onion to taste
2 tablespoons brandy
2 anchovies, chopped
salt to taste
freshly ground pepper to taste

Please note that suggested quantities of ingredients are arbitrary and can be altered according to taste.

Combine butter with mustard and spread on cocktail bread slices. Combine remaining ingredients and mix thoroughly. Mound on bread slices and score all over with tines of a fork.

Makes 16–24, depending on size of bread.

SUGGESTED GARNISH: Rolled anchovy fillet topped with 3 capers or half hard-cooked-egg slice and a few capers.

ENGLISH POTTED SHRIMP ON
TOAST SQUARES

1½ sticks butter
generous pinch mace
generous pinch nutmeg, or more to taste
cayenne pepper to taste
1 cup fresh cooked, shelled, and cut-up
     shrimp, or canned and drained tiny shrimp
hot toast squares

Make clarified butter (see Index). In a saucepan combine about ⅓ of the clarified butter with the mace, nutmeg, and cayenne pepper. Add shrimp and toss gently but thoroughly. Heat over a low flame for a few minutes. Spoon mixture into 2 small crocks, ramekins, or custard cups and pat down to make the tops even. Spoon remaining clarified butter over the shrimps to seal them in. Cool, cover, and refrigerate 8 hours or longer before serving. This can be made a few days in advance.

Before cocktail time, bring the little pots of shrimp to room temperature. Serve with piping-hot toast squares.

Makes enough for 16 or more toast squares.

NIPPY PICKAPEPPA SANDWICHES

1 3-ounce package cream cheese
1 teaspoon (more or less, to taste) Pickapeppa
    Sauce
24 thin whole wheat bread rounds
1 bunch watercress, washed, leaves removed
    and dried thoroughly
softened butter or margarine

Cream the cream cheese, add the Pickapeppa Sauce, and beat until creamy. Spread on half of the bread rounds. Arrange a triple layer of watercress leaves over the cream cheese. Butter remaining bread rounds and place on top of watercress, buttered side down. Wrap in plastic wrap or aluminum foil and chill half an hour or so before serving.

Makes 12.

CASPIAN CAVIAR TOASTS

6 slices firm white bread ¼ inch thick (such as
    Pepperidge Farm Very Thin White Bread)
2 tablespoons butter or margarine, softened
⅛ teaspoon grated lemon peel
pinch of salt
dash of freshly ground pepper
1 finely chopped hard-cooked egg
3 teaspoons caviar (fresh or regular beluga or
    sevruga caviar or lumpfish caviar)

Toast bread slices and cut out 24 circles 1½ inches in diameter with a biscuit cutter. With a thimble or other small round object, cut centers from half of the bread circles, as though cutting holes from doughnuts. Discard the small circles.

Cream butter with lemon peel, salt, and pepper. Add egg and mix well. Spread mixture on the 12 solid bread circles, dividing equally. Place remaining circles on top. Spoon ¼ teaspoon caviar in the hole in the center of each sandwich.

Makes 12.

GARDEN CUCUMBER SANDWICHES

Nothing could be easier or more tempting than cucumber sandwiches made with the produce from your own garden or that of a generous neighbor. If you have to resort to store-bought cucumbers the sandwiches will still be good and refreshing, even if they lack the right-off-the-vine flavor of freshly picked cucumbers.

well-chilled cucumbers
Swedish Lympa Bread (bought or see Index)
   or dark pumpernickel, thinly sliced
mayonnaise
freshly ground pepper
salt

Slice cucumbers about ⅜ inch thick. Cut bread rounds the same size as cucumber rounds and spread with mayonnaise. Lay a cucumber round on the mayonnaise. Sprinkle lightly with pepper and salt. Garnish if desired, and serve immediately, before cucumbers start to weep.

SUGGESTED GARNISH: If you have mint growing in your garden, garnish each sandwich with a tiny mint leaf. Otherwise, garnish with a chive ring or a light sprinkling of finely chopped parsley.

10. SANDWICHES FOR TEATIME

Polly put the kettle on, we'll all have tea.
—CHARLES DICKENS, *Barnaby Rudge*

Afternoon tea may not be an everyday event in your life, but when you do have a tea party or afternoon meeting it can be a lovely and gracious occasion. Fortunately, the era of eating tea sandwiches with gloved fingers has passed into history, but, just as fortunately, the practice of serving dainty tidbits with tea remains.

Tea sandwiches are probably the simplest of all sandwiches to make. They can be prepared ahead of time, are inexpensive, and are delightful morsels to serve with tea. Accompany any tea sandwiches with a plate of nice cookies or small pastries.

Should you happen to own some bone china tea-cups, teatime is probably the only opportunity you have to show them off. Be sure to make the tea properly, though, so the tea and the cup complement both each other and the sandwiches. Heat the teapot first with boiling water, empty and dry it, and then spoon in one teaspoon of loose tea per cup of water. Allow it to steep 3–5 minutes before pouring. Some people prefer to spoon loose tea into a tea ball or use tea bags in place of loose tea. Use a good brand of tea, such as Twinings or Jacksons of Piccadilly, which are readily available in supermarkets as well as specialty food stores, and buy any type that appeals to you. Some of the most popular types are Earl Grey, a lightly scented tea very appropriate at tea time, a China tea such as Formosa Oolong, and an Indian tea such as Darjeeling. You may prefer to serve an herb tea, such as linden or peppermint, which can be found in grocery stores and supermarkets, or one of the many mixtures of herb teas available in specialty food stores and health-food stores. You may even prefer to serve hot chocolate.

But whatever you pour into the cups, be sure to have tea sandwiches to put on the plates. Allow about 4 or 5 sandwiches for each person, or more if you plan to serve very few cookies or pastries with them. Although it may not rank as a sandwich, cinnamon toast is a natural to serve with tea. Simply make it as you would make ordinary cinnamon toast, trim the crusts, and cut into small pieces.

There are some simple general rules for making tea sandwiches which apply to all the following ideas and recipes. Use firm unsliced bread. If the bread happens to be a day or two old, so much the better.

Freshly baked bread will not do, except for rolled sand-wiches. Some breads in this book that are good for tea sandwiches are Wheat Germ Bread, Oatmeal Bread, Southern Potato Bread, Cheddar Cheese Bread, Four Grain Bread, Saffron Bread, Challah, Irish Seedy Bread, Herb Bread, Swedish Lympa Bread, Black Peasant Bread, Banana Bread, Pumpkin Bread, Orange Sunflower Seed Bread, Pecan Bread, and Apple Honey Date Bread (see Index). If you are buying bread for tea sandwiches, buy it unsliced. Some good choices are firm white bread, gingerbread, Boston brown bread, or any bread of firm grain.

To start making tea sandwiches, first slice the bread thinly and spread with softened sweet butter, or try the easier method of buttering the bread and then slicing it off the loaf. Next trim the crusts. Spread with whatever filling you choose, making certain you spread the filling right to the edges all around, cover with buttered bread of same size, and then cut into squares, triangles, or fingers. (If you want to use a cookie cutter for cutting out various sandwich shapes, you'll probably want to cut out the shapes before buttering and spreading with filling, in order to avoid waste of both butter and filling.)

Generally, a loaf of bread will make about 36 thin slices, or about 18 full-size sandwiches. When cut into quarters they will yield 72 tea sandwiches. If you cut them into other shapes the quantity will vary. Sizes of bread loaves vary, too, so that fruit bread, for example, yields fewer slices and smaller slices than Saffron Bread or other large loaves.

Sandwich butters on some of the breads above can stand alone as fillings without further embellishment.

Bread-and-butter sandwiches are a teatime tradition, in fact. Some sandwich butters (see Index) that are particularly appropriate are:

> anchovy butter
> egg yolk–lemon butter
> mint butter
> mixed herb butter
> nut butter
> olive butter
> Parmesan butter
> pickle-pimiento butter
> Roquefort butter
> tarragon, basil, oregano, marjoram, dill, rosemary, or sage butter

These butters can also be used with a filling, but make certain you do not have too many flavors in one sandwich, which might tend to make for confusing tastes. One cup of sandwich butter is sufficient for 8–10 full-size closed sandwiches before being cut into quarters or other shapes.

In addition to the sandwich shapes already mentioned, you can also make the following:

Pinwheels: Slice uncut loaf of fresh bread lengthwise and trim crusts. Butter and spread with filling. Roll up, starting at the long side. Anchor with two or more toothpicks, wrap tightly in plastic wrap, and chill well. At serving time remove toothpicks and cut bread crosswise in slices 1/4–1/3 inch.

Cornucopias: Spread 2½-inch-square trimmed fresh bread slices with butter. Shape into cornucopia shapes and fasten each with a toothpick. Place on baking sheet and heat in 375° oven until lightly toasted. Cool and remove toothpicks. Fill with desired filling at serving time.

Rolled Sandwiches: Trim crusts from fresh soft bread. Spread with butter and filling, roll up, and wrap each tightly in plastic wrap. Chill well. When serving, decorate by inserting a tiny sprig of parsley in each end.

Two-Tone Sandwiches: Use different color breads for the tops and the bottoms of the sandwiches.

Mosaic Sandwiches: Using a dark bread and a light bread, cut equal amounts of squares, circles, hearts, or other shapes from each. Spread butter and any desired filling on half of the dark and half of the light shapes. With a smaller cutter of the same shape, cut centers from remaining pieces. Insert a dark center into light-bread holes and vice versa. Place mosaic pieces of bread on top of the spread bread pieces, putting a dark top on a light bottom and vice versa.

If you are making closed tea sandwiches, which will usually be the case, make them and wrap them in plastic wrap so they do not dry out. Refrigerate until serving time. If you are making open-faced tea sandwiches you will generally have to put the filling on just before you serve them; otherwise they may tend to discolor or stick to plastic wrap when you want to serve them.

Many of the recipes in other chapters of this book are appropriate for conversion into tea sandwiches; some are listed below (see Index). Unless otherwise noted, slice bread thinly as mentioned above, spread with butter and filling, making closed sandwiches, and cut into small squares, triangles, or fingers.

Apple-Date-Chestnut Sandwich

cashew butter (spread on any type bread desired)

Dansk Smørrebrød (make on small scale and serve open-faced)

Fran's Prize-winning Chopped Chicken Liver on Bialy (omit bialys and spread the chilled chopped chicken liver in sandwiches of thinly sliced firm white bread. The chopped liver can be thinned with mayonnaise if desired.)

Garden Cucumber Sandwiches (make open-faced or closed)

Ginger Pumpkin Sandwich

Golden Tongue Sandwich

Irish Seedy Bread Bacon Sandwich

Lashing Tongue Sandwich

Mini Croque Monsieur (make as directed in recipe)

Nippy Pickapeppa Sandwich (make as directed in recipe)

Nutty Seedy Sandwich

Peanut Butter Lemon Marmalade Banana Bread Sandwich

Ricotta Caponata Canapé (use thinly sliced untoasted bread)

Saffron Toast Cottage Cheese Sandwich (make open-faced or closed)

Smoked Turkey Breast on Tomato Bread Sandwich

Stars and Stripes (slice finished loaf thinly and cut slices in half from top to bottom. Serve with cake server or similar flat server.)

Taramosalata Toasts (use thin bread slices instead of toast)

Vitamin C Sandwich

Waffled Soho Sandwich (make as directed and cut into quarters)
Walnutwiches (use untoasted bread)
Zippy Edam Sandwich

Some quick ideas for other tea sandwiches are:

Pumpkin Bread (see Index) spread with butter and filled with Port Salut or Bel Paese cheese cut to fit

Orange Sunflower Seed Bread (see Index) spread with butter and filled with cream cheese topped by orange marmalade

Banana Bread (see Index) spread with butter and filled with cottage cheese and chopped raisins

Pecan Bread (see Index) spread with butter and filled with farmer cheese and apricot preserves

Wheat Germ Bread (bought or see Index) spread with Parmesan butter (see Index) and filled with shredded buttery-type lettuce

Any firm bread spread with a prepared filling from a jar or can, such as lobster spread, crab spread, or canned pâté which has been softened and thinned with a little mayonnaise

The following recipes for tea sandwich fillings can be made with any firm-type buttered bread you like.

Chicken Tea Sandwich Filling: Combine 1 cup finely chopped cooked chicken, ½ cup finely chopped walnuts, 2 teaspoons Dijon mustard, and enough mayonnaise to moisten. Cover and refrigerate until ready to make sandwiches.

Roquefort-Avocado Tea Sandwich Filling: Mash together ¼ cup crumbled Roquefort cheese and 1 cup avocado purée. Add 1 tablespoon lemon juice and make sandwiches immediately.

Sardine Tea Sandwich Filling: Force through a coarse sieve, or put through food processor or blender without allowing mixture to become puréed: 1 can sardines, well drained, 2 coarsely chopped hard-cooked eggs, 3 tablespoons softened butter, 1 teaspoon grated lemon peel, 1 tablespoon lemon juice, ½ teaspoon grated union, ½ teaspoon salt, and freshly ground pepper to taste. Cover and refrigerate until ready to make sandwiches.

FRUIT AND DATE TEA SANDWICH FILLING

½ cup each pitted dates, pitted prunes, raisins
(Monukka raisins if available), dried
apricots, dried black Mission figs*, dried
Calimyrna figs*
½ orange, sliced and seeded
½ lemon, sliced and seeded
1¼ cups water
fruit juice as needed

* If this type fig is not available, use any type dried fig that is available.

Combine all ingredients except fruit juice in a saucepan, bring to boil, lower heat, cover, and simmer until water is absorbed. Uncover and allow to cool. Put through meat grinder fitted with medium blade. Mix thoroughly and pack into a 2½-cup jar. Refrigerate until an hour or so before making sandwiches with thinly sliced bread. White or other light bread is preferable. If filling is too thick to spread, thin with fruit juice. Filling will keep at least a month tightly capped and refrigerated.

Makes about 2½ cups.

CREAM CHEESE TEA SANDWICH FILLINGS

1 3-ounce package cream cheese
1 tablespoon or more milk or cream

For each flavor filling use one of the following:
½ cup chopped salted pistachios or almonds
¼ cup chopped green olives
3 tablespoons cooked, drained, crumbled bacon
½ cup finely chopped mushrooms, ½
    teaspoon grated onion, salt and freshly
    ground pepper to taste
2 tablespoons currant jam or other jam
    (not jelly)

Soften cream cheese and thin with milk or cream to spreading consistency. Add flavoring and make sandwiches immediately.

CHOPPED EGG TEA SANDWICH FILLINGS

2 chopped hard-cooked eggs
1 teaspoon lemon juice
¼ teaspoon salt
freshly ground pepper to taste
2 or more tablespoons mayonnaise

For each flavor filling use one of the following:
6 or more pimiento-stuffed olives, finely
    chopped
½ cup finely chopped pecans and
    ¼ teaspoon Worcestershire sauce
4 finely chopped anchovies and ¼ cup finely
    chopped celery
⅓ cup finely chopped cooked shrimp
    marinated in oil-and-vinegar dressing for
    1 hour
1 small can deviled ham and ½ teaspoon
    horseradish
1 small can liver pâté

Combine egg, lemon juice, salt, pepper, and enough mayonnaise for spreading consistency. Add flavoring and combine well. If not using immediately, cover and refrigerate until needed.

SANDWICH ISLAND TEA SANDWICH FILLING

Long before we knew them as the Hawaiian Islands, the pineapple-producing paradise was known as the Sandwich Islands, after the fourth Earl of Sandwich. This pineapple teatime treat is in honor of the islands—and the Earl.

> 1 3-ounce package cream cheese
> ½ cup chilled crushed pineapple, drained
>   (reserve juice)
> ¼ cup chopped macadamia nuts or walnuts
> ¼ cup chopped black olives

Cream the cream cheese and add pineapple gradually. Add nuts and olives and mix well. If mixture is too stiff to spread, thin slightly with some of the reserved pineapple juice. Cover and refrigerate until needed, or make sandwiches immediately.

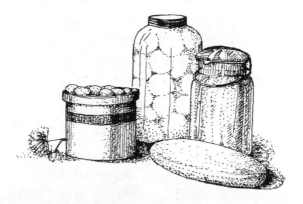

11. GREAT SANDWICH GARNISHES AND ACCOMPANIMENTS

See they be garnished fair.
—FRANCIS THOMPSON, *from The Night of Forebeing; Ode to Easter*

This is a chapter of extras to set your sandwiches off to best advantage. There are instructions for making vegetable garnishes, a discussion of ready-made pickles and chutneys, as well as recipes for making some of the more unusual ones yourself, recipes for other sandwich accompaniments and salads, and a few useful dressing and sauce recipes you will probably want to refer to when making several of the sandwiches in this book.

VEGETABLE GARNISHES FOR SANDWICHES

Use these garnishes either by arranging them on each plate alongside or on top of a sandwich, or by decorating a whole platter of sandwiches with them. The radish roses and tomato roses are best used as decorations on platters of sandwiches, and the cucumber cups are generally more suitable for individual plates. Olives, both green and black, look attractive with many of these vegetable garnishes.

Pickle Fans: With a sharp knife cut gherkins or any cucumber pickle into thin parallel slices almost the length of the pickle. Spread out into fan shape and press the uncut end between thumb and forefinger to retain fan shape.

Cucumber Twists: Slice cucumber very thin. Slash each slice to the center in one place. Twist one cut side up and the other down and around, spreading out the cucumber as much as possible.

Cucumber Cups: Cut small cucumbers in half lengthwise and scoop out seeds. Fill hollow with olives, pickles, or any desired condiment, or other raw vegetables.

Radish Fans: With a sharp knife cut oval radishes crosswise into thin parallel slices without cutting all the way through. Place in ice water several hours to allow radishes to fan out.

Carrot Curls: With a vegetable peeler cut thin lengthwise slices from a peeled carrot. Roll up into curls and put in ice water to crisp.

Radish Roses: Trim off roots and stems of radishes. Starting from the root end, peel the skin away from the radish in 5 or 6 places, cutting down almost to the bottom of the radish to form petals. If you can manage it, a second row of petals can be cut inside the first. Put in ice water to open petals and crisp the radishes.

Scallions: Trim off root and cut the green part off so that the scallion is about 1½ inches long. Remove outer layer of scallion if not clean and unblemished. Cut straight down through the stalk to the top of the bulb several times to form a fringe. Put in ice water to open the fringe.

Carrot Trees: Cut peeled carrot in half lengthwise. Lay flat side down. Cut parallel slits halfway down the length of each carrot half. Put in ice water to open branches and crisp the carrots.

Celery Trees: Make in the same manner as carrot trees, above, using inner small celery ribs.

Tomato Roses: Pare the skin of a ripe tomato, including a little of the pulp, in a single band, going round and round from top to bottom of tomato without trying to keep the strip even. Roll the strip into a rosette. Stems and/or leaves for the rose can be made from scallions, leeks, or celery.

Flat Radish Flowers: Trim off roots and stems from large perfectly shaped radishes. Slice as thinly as possible and arrange 8–10 overlapping slices in a circle to form a flat flower. For flower center cut a tiny circle of red part of radish, unwaxed cucumber skin, zucchini skin, or carrot, using an hors d'oeuvre or truffle cutter or point of a small sharp knife. Place in center of flower.

PICKLES AND CHUTNEYS

It's debatable which is the sandwich's best friend, the mustard or the pickle, and ultimately it seems they should share equal billing. There are so many delightful pickles to accompany sandwiches that you can have a different one every day of the month without repeating and without coming to the end of a seemingly inexhaustible variety. Since there are so many good pickles available in stores, I'll discuss these before giving recipes for some of the more unusual ones that you may want to try making yourself. (If you get hooked on the idea of pickle making, there are many magazine articles on how to do it each year in late summer, and a number of good books to which you can refer for other ideas.)

Dilly beans, which are green beans pickled in dill vinegar, are one of America's contributions to pickledom, and are especially nice with fish and seafood sandwiches. England is probably best known for its pickled walnuts, pickled mushrooms, and pickled onions, given a special tang by the use of malt vinegar. All are available in specialty food stores and many supermarkets, and are very good with meat sandwiches. Kimchi, which is Korean pickled cabbage, is a pickle like no other, and not for the faint of heart. But if you like something really out of the ordinary, try it with your next hearty sandwich. You can buy kimchi in little cans in Oriental or specialty food stores.

Germany has probably produced a greater variety of pickles than any other country in the world, and many of these are obtainable here. "Sour makes cheerful," says an old German proverb, and these sweet-sour creations are cheerful companions to sandwiches. Some of the more interesting ones are senfgurken (peeled cucumber pickles flavored with ginger, dill, and mustard seed), pickled baby corn, kraut salad, gherkins, pickled pumpkin, pearl onions, and mixed pickles containing cauliflower, gherkins or cucumber slices, pearl onions, carrot slices, beans, and pieces of celery knob. The most distinct French pickles are cornichons, which are vinegar-and-spice-marinated midget gherkins about half the size of your pinky, with not a trace of sugar in them. Poland ships over some excellent dill pickles.

How many varieties of pickles Heinz is making these days is beyond me—nor do I know how many other companies there are making just as many or more kinds—but a look on the grocer's shelf and through the glass at the delicatessen counter reveals the availability of all kinds of cucumber pickles, ranging from kosher dills to sweet bread-and-butter slices, and icicle pickles, cauliflower pickles, chow-chow and other mustard pickles, pickled onions, pickled watermelon rind, pickled crabapples, pickled peaches, relishes such as corn relish and India relish, and many more.

If you like pickles with your sandwiches you probably adore chutney, and it's worth exploring for something besides the ever-reliable Major Grey's. Apple chutney is nice, and there are many mango chutneys, both mild and hot, that go well with sandwiches. Chutney can be found in specialty food stores and Indian food markets, which also carry whole lemon pickles and other rarities, as well as in many grocery stores and some supermarkets.

Recipes for some other out-of-the-ordinary chutneys follow the pickle recipes in this chapter.

PETER PIPER'S FRESH PICKLED SWEET GREEN PEPPERS

4 large green bell peppers
1 carrot, peeled and cut into 3- or 4-inch
    lengths, then each piece cut in quarters
    lengthwise
1 small hot red pepper, seeds removed, cut
    into strips
1 garlic clove, bruised
⅔ cup water
1⅓ cups white vinegar
1 bay leaf
10 peppercorns
½ teaspoon salt
1 tablespoon brown sugar

With a long fork, hold peppers, one at a time, over
high flame or over highest setting of electric stove
burner, turning until skins blister all over. Rinse under
cold running water and set aside until all peppers have
been blistered. Peel off skins with the aid of a small
sharp knife. Cut around cores and remove. Cut peppers
in half lengthwise. Cut away membranes and remove
seeds. Rinse under cold running water.

Pack peppers into a wide-mouthed 1-quart jar,
along with the carrot and red pepper pieces, tucking
the garlic clove into the middle of the jar. Combine
remaining ingredients in small saucepan and bring to a
boil. Stir to dissolve sugar. Cool slightly and pour over
peppers in jar, tucking the bay leaf into side of jar.
Cover tightly. Cool and refrigerate overnight or up to 2
weeks before serving.

Makes 8 servings as a sandwich accompaniment.

PINEAPPLE PICKLES

1 large pineapple
whole cloves
⅔ cup white vinegar
5 tablespoons lemon juice
½ teaspoon salt
½ teaspoon black peppercorns

Peel and core pineapple. Cut into 1-inch slices. Cut slices into chunks about 1 inch wide. Stick a clove into every other chunk. Put chunks in a large sterilized jar. Combine remaining ingredients in a saucepan, bring to a boil, and pour over chunks. Cool, seal tightly, and chill.

Makes about 1 quart, depending on size of pineapple.

GINGER-LIME CUCUMBER PICKLES

2 pounds cucumbers (4 medium-size
    cucumbers)
1 tablespoon salt
1½ cups rice vinegar or white vinegar
1 cup sugar
5 tablespoons lime juice
1 cinnamon stick
4 whole cloves
2 tablespoons sliced fresh ginger root or
    canned green ginger root

Peel cucumbers. Cut in quarters lengthwise. Remove and discard seeds. Cut cucumbers into 1-inch lengths. Put in colander and sprinkle all over with salt. Allow to stand 5–10 minutes. Shake to remove liquid.

Combine remaining ingredients in saucepan and bring to boil. Add cucumbers and simmer until they look glassy. With a slotted spoon transfer cucumbers to sterilized jars. Boil down liquid until syrupy. Pour over cucumbers and allow to cool. Seal tightly and chill. Use within a week or two.

Makes about 1 quart.

PICKLED CARROT SLIMS

1 bunch slender carrots
1 slice red onion, cut in half and separated
   into arcs
½ cup white vinegar
½ cup water
⅓ cup sugar
1½ teaspoons mustard seed
½ teaspoon salt
1 teaspoon dill weed

Peel carrots. Cut in half crosswise. Cut into strips less than ⅛ inch thick. Pack upright in a 1-pint jar, along with onion. Combine remaining ingredients in a saucepan and bring to boil, stirring. Pour over carrots. Cool, cap tightly, and chill. Allow to marinate in jar in refrigerator 2 or 3 days before serving.

Makes 1 pint.

PICKLED GRAPES

2 pounds seedless grapes
½ cup white vinegar
1½ cups sugar
2 cardamom seeds (whole pods)
¼ teaspoon mace
¼ teaspoon ginger
¼ teaspoon cinnamon
¼ teaspoon basil

Wash grapes, stem, dry, and cut in half lengthwise. Put remaining ingredients in saucepan. Bring to a boil, stirring, until sugar is dissolved. Boil 6 minutes, covered. Add grapes and cook 3 minutes, until fruit is not quite tender. Pack in hot sterilized jars, dividing fruit and liquid evenly. Seal. Cool and refrigerate. Allow to stand 3 days before serving.

Makes five 1-cup jars.

MOTHER'S GREEN TOMATO PICKLES

8 pounds green tomatoes, sliced ¼ inch
   thick
6 medium onions, sliced
2 sweet red peppers, cut in small pieces
cold water
salt (not iodized salt or rock salt)
¼ cup mixed pickling spices
3 cups vinegar
3 cups water
2 cups brown sugar, firmly packed
1 teaspoon cinnamon
½ teaspoon cloves
½ teaspoon allspice

Combine tomato slices, onion slices, and red peppers in a glass or ceramic bowl. Combine cold water and salt in the proportion of 1 cup salt to 2 quarts water, and pour enough of this brine over the vegetables to cover. Allow to stand 10–12 hours.

Drain and rinse well with cold water. Tie mixed pickling spices in clean cheesecloth and drop into a pot. Add vinegar, 3 cups water, and sugar, cinnamon, cloves, and allspice. Bring to a boil, stirring until sugar is dissolved. Boil about 3 minutes. Add tomato mixture and bring to a boil again. Boil just a few minutes, to heat through thoroughly. Remove spice bag and transfer pickles and liquid to sterilized jars. Spoon a thin layer of melted paraffin over top of each jar. When set, spoon on another layer of paraffin. Seal and store in a cool place.

Makes about 3 quarts.

INDONESIAN PICKLE MIXTURE
Atjar Tjampur

2 garlic cloves

3 macadamia nuts

½ teaspoon turmeric

½ teaspoon ginger

1 teaspoon salt

1 tablespoon vegetable oil

1½ cups white vinegar

5 tablespoons lemon or lime juice

1 tablespoon sugar

½ teaspoon sambal ulek* or crushed red
   pepper flakes

¼ pound green beans, cut in ¼-inch slices

¼ pound carrots, peeled and cut in thin
   short strips

1½ cups shredded cabbage

¾ cup tiny cauliflower florets

¼ pound fresh bean sprouts or drained
   canned bean sprouts

½ cup peeled, seeded cucumber cut into
   small cubes

2 chilies, seeds removed, cut into small
   pieces

* Raw hot chilies which have been crushed with salt. Available in specialty food stores which carry Indonesian products. Conimex, imported from Holland, is the brand most frequently seen.

Crush into a paste with mortar and pestle, or put through blender or food processor with a little oil until completely pulverized, the garlic, nuts, turmeric, ginger, and salt. Sauté in oil over medium heat for 2 minutes, stirring constantly. Do not allow to scorch or burn.

Remove from heat. Add vinegar, lemon juice, sugar, and sambal ulek or red pepper flakes, and transfer to large saucepan. Add green beans and carrots and simmer until half cooked. Add cabbage and cauliflower and simmer until cauliflower is half cooked. Add remaining ingredients and simmer 2 minutes more. Remove from stove. Cool and pour into large sterile jar. Seal and chill. Serve as a relish.

Makes 1 large jar.

ORANGE–PICKLED WALNUT CHUTNEY

3½ cups or more malt vinegar, or use part
    vinegar and part liquid from pickled
    walnuts, below
1 12-ounce package pitted ready-to-eat
    prunes
1 12-ounce package pitted dates, chopped
3 pounds firm tart apples, cored and
    coarsely chopped
4 cups peeled and coarsely chopped onions
4 oranges (any kind but navel oranges)
1 lemon
2 cups dark brown sugar
8–10 pickled walnuts,* drained and
    crushed
4 garlic cloves, bruised
1½ ounces mixed pickling spices

---

* Pickled walnuts, which come from England, can be found in specialty food stores, grocery stores, and in the pickle section or "gourmet" section of supermarkets.

Bring 1½ cups vinegar to a boil. Add prunes and simmer 5 minutes, covered. Set aside while preparing and chopping dates, apples, and onions. Drain prunes, reserving vinegar in which they were boiled.

Combine prunes, dates, apples, and onions in a pot. Cut off any stamping on oranges and lemons. Cut each in several pieces, removing seeds and stem ends. Put pieces through a food processor until quite coarse, or put through a meat grinder fitted with a coarse blade. Measure reserved vinegar and add more vinegar to measure 3½ cups. Add to prune mixture along with sugar and walnuts. Tie garlic and pickling spices in clean cloth and drop into pot. Bring mixture to boil and simmer until apples have disintegrated, 3–3½ hours, stirring often. Remove garlic and spice bag. Pack chutney in sterilized jars. Seal, cool, and refrigerate. Allow to mellow at least 1 week before serving.

Makes 3½ quarts.

CRANBERRY CHUTNEY

1 pound fresh cranberries

2 green apples, peeled, cored, and finely
chopped

1½ oranges (any kind but navel oranges),
thinly sliced, quartered, and seeds
removed

1 cup dark brown sugar

1 cup cider vinegar

4 ounces drained preserved ginger,* diced
(scant ⅔ cup)

4 ounces candied lemon peel (generous
¾ cup)

2 garlic cloves, chopped

6 whole cloves

6 allspice berries

1 tablespoon curry powder

1 teaspoon salt

¼ teaspoon mustard seed

* Preserved ginger comes in a jar, generally of about 7 ounces, packed in
syrup. (The syrup makes good dessert flavoring.)

Combine all ingredients in pot and bring to boil.
Lower heat and simmer for 15 minutes or until
thickened, stirring frequently. Pack in sterilized jars.
Spoon a thin layer of melted paraffin over top of each
jar. When set, spoon on another layer of paraffin. Seal,
cool, and store in a cool place to mellow 1–4 weeks before serving.

Makes 3 cups.

DRESSINGS AND SALADS

VINAIGRETTE DRESSING

Some call it oil-and-vinegar dressing, others Italian dressing or French dressing, and still others vinaigrette. No matter what you call it, it's simply a basic oil-and-vinegar dressing that you can use on salads and for marinating vegetables. What makes a really good vinaigrette is the oil and vinegar you choose. It's worth the money to buy some French red wine or white tarragon vinegar. It costs only pennies per salad and makes such a difference. Oil is a matter of personal preference. Some like olive oil, others a mixture of olive and another oil. There are several light French and Italian virgin olive oils that do not overwhelm you as some heavier oils can. Equally good things can be said about safflower, sunflower, peanut, soy bean, and wheat germ oils, used alone or in a mixture of two or three. Don't forget that freshly ground pepper and freshly ground salt or kosher salt make any salad dressing sparkle.

There is great controversy and difference of opinion about proportions of oil to vinegar. I like a higher proportion of vinegar than the old-fashioned standard of 4 parts oil to 1 part vinegar, so my recipe goes accordingly. But change the proportions to suit yourself if you like a less tart, or even more tart, taste. You can also substitute lemon juice for part of the vinegar if you like.

½ cup oil

3 tablespoons wine vinegar

1 teaspoon salt

freshly ground pepper to taste

1 teaspoon dry mustard or prepared Dijon
   mustard

½ teaspoon tarragon, basil, or chervil
   and/or pinch of thyme, or any herbs to
   taste

Shake all ingredients together in a bottle, or whisk all ingredients except oil together in a small bowl, then whisk in the oil. If you want to include garlic, rub the bowl with it, mince a little very finely and add it to whatever you are preparing, or add it to the vinaigrette itself if you plan to use it all at once. Garlic left in vinaigrette tends to take on an unpleasant taste. Alternatively, add chopped shallots, scallions, or chives to whatever you are preparing, in place of garlic.

Makes about ¾ cup.

RUSSIAN DRESSING

½ cup mayonnaise
1 tablespoon ketchup
2 tablespoons chopped sour pickle
1 tablespoon chopped parsley
1 teaspoon snipped chives
1 tablespoon chopped pimiento
½ teaspoon horseradish
¼ teaspoon Worcestershire sauce

Stir mayonnaise until smooth. Add remaining ingredients and mix well. Store in tightly sealed glass jar in refrigerator if not using immediately.

Makes about ¾ cup.

HORSERADISH DRESSING

½ cup heavy cream
3 tablespoons lemon juice
¼ teaspoon salt
freshly ground pepper (preferably white
    pepper) to taste
2 tablespoons horseradish
1 teaspoon finely chopped scallion

Beat heavy cream until stiff. Add lemon juice gradually, beating constantly. Stir in remaining ingredients. If not serving immediately, cover and refrigerate. Stir before serving, as the mixture will separate on standing. Use as directed in individual recipe, or on meat sandwiches. Especially nice with cold roast beef sandwiches. Makes about 1¼ cups.

DELI SALAD

6 cups finely shredded cabbage
1½ cups shredded carrot
½ cup chopped green pepper
⅔ cup water
⅔ cup white vinegar
¼ cup sugar
1 teaspoon salt
pimiento-stuffed olives and pickled herring
    pieces (optional garnishes)

Toss vegetables together. Combine water, vinegar, sugar, and salt, stirring until sugar is dissolved. Pour over vegetables and toss. Cover and refrigerate several hours or overnight, stirring and turning occasionally.

Garnish with halved olives and herring pieces before serving if desired.

Makes about 8 servings.

ITALIAN SALAD

¾ cup cooked peas
¾ cup cooked diced carrots
1½ cups cooked elbow macaroni,
    preferably whole wheat elbow macaroni
⅓ cup sliced pitted black olives,
    preferably Greek or Italian
⅓ cup mayonnaise
1 tablespoon lemon juice
freshly ground pepper to taste

Combine peas, carrots, macaroni, and olives. Combine mayonnaise, lemon juice, and pepper, and pour over the vegetable and macaroni mixture. Toss lightly. Cover and chill before serving.

Makes 4 servings.

BENNETTA'S ARTICHOKE-RICE SALAD

1 cup rice
chicken broth
3 tablespoons chopped scallion, including
      some of green part
2 tablespoons finely chopped green pepper
2 tablespoons sliced pimiento-stuffed olives
1 large jar marinated artichokes, drained
      (reserve marinade) and cut in half
      lengthwise
1/3 cup mayonnaise
juice of 1 lemon
1/2 teaspoon curry powder, or to taste

Cook rice in enough boiling chicken broth to cover by 1 inch until just tender, being careful not to overcook. Cool, fluff, cover, and chill.

Toss rice with scallions, green pepper, olives, and artichokes.

Combine mayonnaise with lemon juice. Add some of the reserved artichoke marinade so that the dressing is fairly liquid. Add curry powder and combine. Toss with the rice mixture.

Makes 4–6 servings.

SHREDDED BEET SALAD

¼ cup mayonnaise
¼ cup sour cream
3 cups cooked shredded beets or canned
    shoestring beets, drained
2 hard-cooked eggs, chopped
3 thin slices (or to taste) onion
1 teaspoon chopped fresh dill, or ½
    teaspoon dill weed
½ teaspoon salt
freshly ground pepper to taste

Combine mayonnaise and sour cream. Toss beets, eggs, onion, dill, salt, and pepper together. Add mayonnaise mixture and mix lightly. Cover and chill.

Makes 6 servings.

WHITE SALAD

2 cucumbers, peeled and thinly sliced
4 cups thinly sliced cauliflower florets
Bermuda onion to taste, sliced paper-thin
    and broken into rings
⅔ cup sour cream
1 tablespoon vinegar
2 teaspoons horseradish
1½ teaspoons salt
white pepper to taste
4–6 endives, broken into leaves

Combine cucumber, cauliflower, and onion. Combine sour cream, vinegar, horseradish, salt, and white pepper, and toss with the vegetables. Cover and chill well. Toss and taste for seasoning, correcting if necessary. Serve in bowl lined with endive.

Makes 8 servings.

ROBERT'S SHREDDED CARROTS
VINAIGRETTE

1 bunch carrots
1 tablespoon chopped scallion
2 tablespoons chopped parsley
1 teaspoon chopped fresh dill (optional)
vinaigrette dressing (see Index) or other
**   oil-and-vinegar dressing**

Peel or scrape carrots and shred coarsely. Combine with remaining ingredients, using enough dressing to moisten. Cover and chill before serving.

Makes 4–6 servings.

CRUNCHY DANISH CUCUMBER SALAD

3 cucumbers, peeled and sliced paper-thin
1 tablespoon plus 1 teaspoon salt
1 cup white vinegar
½ cup water
½ cup sugar
freshly ground pepper to taste

Arrange cucumber slices in colander and sprinkle all over with 1 tablespoon salt, tossing well. Allow to stand 30 minutes.

Squeeze cucumbers to remove as much moisture as possible. This is easiest if you put the cucumbers in a piece of clean cheesecloth before squeezing them.

Combine vinegar, water, sugar, remaining salt, and pepper in a bowl. Add cucumber. Toss, cover, and chill 3–4 hours. Drain and serve. Makes 5–6 servings.

FLORINDA'S OLIVE SALAD

1 pound green Spanish olives with pits
3 or 4 ribs celery, diced
1 onion, thinly sliced
1 cup grated or shredded carrot
salt to taste
freshly ground pepper to taste
red wine vinegar

Crack olives, one at a time, on a board with a kitchen mallet or steak tenderizer. Discard pits and put olives in a bowl. Add celery, onion, and carrot, and toss. Add salt, pepper, and just enough vinegar to moisten, and toss again. Set a plate directly on top of the olive mixture inside the bowl, and set a weight or heavy object on the plate. Cover the bowl with plastic wrap and refrigerate 16–24 hours before serving.

Makes 10 or more servings.

FLAGEOLET SALAD

2 cups dried flageolets,* 2 quarts water, and
   1 tablespoon salt, or 2 15-ounce cans
   cooked green flageolets, drained and
   rinsed
¼ cup scallion, including some of green
   part, finely chopped
¼ cup vinaigrette dressing (see Index) or
   any oil-and-vinegar dressing

* Flageolets are small beans that look somewhat like slender baby lima beans, but have a more distinctive flavor and different texture. They can be bought dried or canned in specialty food stores and in some super-markets and grocery stores.

If using dried flageolets, soak in cold water for 2 hours. Replace water with 2 quarts fresh water and add 1 tablespoon salt. Bring to boil and simmer until tender, 1–2 hours. Drain and cool.

Cover and chill beans. Combine chilled flageolets with scallions and vinaigrette dressing and toss well.

Makes 6 servings.

CAPONATA

1½ pounds eggplant (baby eggplants are
   especially nice)
1 tablespoon salt
3 ribs celery
3 medium-size onions
½ cup or more olive oil
1½ pounds tomatoes, peeled, cored,
   seeded, and diced
¼ cup capers
½ cup sliced pitted black olives
2 tablespoons pine nuts (pignolias)
   (optional)
¼ cup red wine vinegar
1 teaspoon sugar
freshly ground pepper to taste

Cut unpeeled eggplant into cubes about ½–¾ inch square. Put in colander, sprinkle with salt, and allow to stand for about half an hour.

Meanwhile, dice celery and chop onions. Sauté them in ½ cup oil in a large skillet over low heat until onions are soft but only slightly browned. Remove from skillet with a slotted spoon.

Pat and squeeze eggplant cubes dry with paper towel and sauté in the oil remaining in the skillet, adding a little more oil if necessary, until lightly browned. Add tomatoes and sautéed onion and celery, and cook over low heat about 10 minutes, stirring often. Add capers, olives, pine nuts, vinegar, sugar, and pepper. Mix well, cover, lower heat, and simmer 15 minutes, stirring occasionally. If mixture becomes too dry, add a few drops of water during cooking. Taste and correct for seasoning. Cool.

Spoon into glass jars or non-plastic bowl. Cover tightly and chill well before serving. This is best made a day or two before you plan to serve it.

Makes about 5 cups. Use as sandwich accompaniment—especially nice with egg sandwiches, sandwiches made on Italian or French bread, and tuna sandwiches.

PICKLED EGGS

6 eggs
1 small can sliced beets
¼ cup vinegar
¼ cup sugar
salt to taste
freshly ground pepper to taste
generous pinch of celery seed
generous pinch of allspice

Hard-cook eggs. Shell and set aside.

Drain beets and reserve liquid. Put beets, vinegar, ¼ cup beet liquid (or beet liquid and enough water to make ¼ cup), sugar, salt, pepper, celery seed, and allspice in a saucepan and bring to boil. Remove from heat and pour into a bowl. Add eggs and allow to cool. Cover and refrigerate 24 hours or more before serving, turning once or twice during that time.

Makes 6 servings as a sandwich accompaniment.

FRENCH-FRIED MUSHROOMS

1 pound fairly small mushrooms
2 eggs
½ cup buttermilk
1 teaspoon salt
cayenne pepper to taste
flour
oil for deep frying

Trim mushrooms and leave whole. Clean and dry if necessary. Beat eggs lightly. Add buttermilk, salt, and cayenne pepper. Transfer mixture to a shallow soup plate. Put some flour in another shallow soup plate.

Heat oil in wok or deep fryer to 375°. Dip mushrooms, one at a time, into buttermilk mixture, then into flour, coating well. Lower into hot oil, 2 or 3 at a time, and fry until golden. Drain on paper towels. Serve immediately.

Makes 6–8 servings as a sandwich accompaniment.

MARINATED MUSHROOM
AVOCADO MÉLANGE

½ pound mushrooms
1 tablespoon chopped parsley
1 small garlic clove, finely minced
¼ cup lemon juice
⅓ cup vegetable oil
1 tablespoon white tarragon vinegar
1 teaspoon salt
freshly ground pepper to taste
2 ripe avocados

Trim mushrooms and slice thinly. Put in bowl with parsley and garlic and toss lightly. Add lemon juice, oil, vinegar, salt, and pepper, and toss again. Peel avocados, cut in half, and remove pits. Cut in ½-inch slices and gently toss with mushroom mixture. Cover tightly and chill 1–6 hours before serving.

Makes 6 servings.

AVGOLEMONO
(Greek Lemon-Egg Soup)

¼ **cup orzo (rice-shaped pasta)**
4 cups chicken broth
2 eggs
juice of 1 lemon

Follow package directions for *al dente* orzo. Drain. Bring chicken broth to a boil.

Meanwhile, beat eggs well. Beat in lemon juice. Add a little of the hot broth. Remove hot broth from stove and add the egg-lemon mixture and cooked orzo to it. Serve immediately, or let cool and reheat later in top of double boiler until very hot, but do not boil.

Makes 8 servings, served in soup cups. Good with almost any kind of sandwich that you want to serve a soup with.

TARTAR SAUCE

1 cup mayonnaise
1 hard-cooked egg yolk, put through fine
   sieve
1 tablespoon finely chopped gherkins or
   pickle relish
1 tablespoon capers
2 teaspoons finely chopped parsley
2 teaspoons finely snipped chives
½ teaspoon fresh or ¼ teaspoon dried
   tarragon

Combine ingredients in order given. Store in tightly sealed glass jar and refrigerate until ready to use.

Makes about 1¼ cups.

BÉCHAMEL SAUCE

2 tablespoons butter
2 tablespoons flour
1 cup milk (or part cream, or light stock)
½ teaspoon salt
freshly ground pepper to taste (preferably
    white pepper)
pinch of nutmeg

Melt butter over low flame. Stir in flour and cook, stirring with wooden spoon, for a minute or two, not allowing it to brown. Remove from heat and add milk or stock all at once, beating in with wire whisk. Cook, stirring with wire whisk, until mixture is thickened and bubbly. Remove from heat and stir in salt, pepper, and nutmeg. Use as directed in individual recipe.

Makes about 1 cup.

MORNAY SAUCE

1 recipe béchamel sauce (above) made with
    milk or milk and cream
½ cup chicken broth
1 tablespoon butter
¼ cup grated Gruyère cheese (not
    processed Gruyère)
¼ cup grated Parmesan cheese

Heat the béchamel sauce with chicken broth to boiling point and simmer a few minutes. Remove from heat and add remaining ingredients, stirring until cheese has melted fairly well. Use as directed in individual recipe. Makes about 1¾ cups.

Index